Murder in Edwardian Merseyside

by
DAVID PARRY

Books of related interest

Liverpool: A People's History (2008)

Liverpool in the sixteenth century: a small Tudor town (2007)

*The Black Widows of Liverpool: a chilling account of
cold-blooded murder in Victorian Liverpool* (second edition, 2009)

Georgian Liverpool: A Guide to the city in 1797 (2007)

Merseyside Murders of the 1920s (2007)

www.carnegiepublishing.com
www.palatinebooks.com

For information about self-publishing see www.scotforthbooks.com

Murder in Edwardian Merseyside
by David Parry

Reprinted 2009

First published in 2005
by Palatine Books,
Carnegie House, Chatsworth Road
Lancaster LA1 4SL
www.palatinebooks.com

British Library Cataloguing-in-Publication data
A catalogue record for this book is available from the British Library

ISBN 10: 1-874181-27-6
ISBN 13: 978-1-874181-27-9

Typeset by Carnegie Book Production, Lancaster
Printed and bound by Cromwell Press Group Ltd

Contents

Introduction

The forty-three murder cases in this book comprise mainly of those which came to trial at the Liverpool Assizes held in St George's Hall, together with a small number of cases from the Cheshire side of the Mersey. They attempt to show the link between crime and poverty in the Edwardian City and how the judicial system operated in the courts. Contemporary background to the cases is provided by highlighted sections within the text.

Acknowledgements

The author wishes to thank all the staff at the William Brown Library, Liverpool for their help in the research for this book. Particular thanks is expressed to Ivan Frontani who provided the line drawings and to Janet McLarney who supplied the background highlights. Thank you also to all those at Carnegie Publishing Ltd who assisted in the preparation of the manuscript for publication.

1901

*Queen Victoria died on 22 January 1901. A new
Edwardian era began with the accession to the throne
of the queen's second child and eldest son 'Bertie',
who became King Edward VII.*

A Dead Child and A Drowned Man

On Tuesday 15 January 1901, Mrs Alma Murray, who lived with her
husband James Murray at 36 Parr Street, was working most of the day in
the public wash house in Frederick Street. She got home at about 4.15 p.m.
and began to prepare a meal in the kitchen. In the house were Mrs
Murray's six-year-old daughter Eveline and David Chapman, a ten-year-old
boy whom she had adopted. At 5.15 p.m., Mrs Murray's lodger came in. He
was John William Bennett, a labourer employed by the corporation. Mr
Murray, an able seaman, was away on a voyage.

When Bennett arrived, he sat down near the fire. He had been drinking but was quite sober. Bennett got out his clay pipe and began to smoke.
Realising there was more laundry to be done, Mrs Murray decided to send
young David on ahead to the wash house and she followed him. Little
Eveline asked her mother for her tea and Mrs Murray told her she would
be back home soon.

Mrs Murray stayed at the wash house until 6.15 p.m. David brought her
some clothes and she told him to go home and put the kettle on the fire.
David got home at about 6.10 p.m. Finding the front door shut, he knocked
several times, but got no answer. Looking through the keyhole, the boy saw
Bennett open the kitchen door and go up the steps into the yard. He had
a parcel wrapped in newspaper under his arm. Bennett closed the kitchen
door after himself and David shouted Eveline's name but there was no
answer. He looked through the keyhole again. This time, David saw

Bennett come back from the yard into the kitchen, still carrying the parcel. Bennett walked to the front door, opened it, and said 'Hello David.'

Eveline was nowhere to be seen. The parlour door had been broken open and a money box and a carving knife lay on the kitchen table. David ran to tell his mother. Mrs Murray saw him running up to her as she was coming home and he told her what he had seen at the house. Just then, a man ran past whom Mrs Murray thought was Bennett. On entering the house, she found things as David had described. The contents of the kitchen were all upset and little Eveline could not be found. At about 7.30 p.m., Mrs Murray went into the yard where she saw a pool of blood. Now desperate, she went to the police office for help.

At 9.45 p.m. that night, Detective Sub-Inspector Gibbons went with Constable Howell to 36 Parr Street. They were shown the blood in the yard and they began a fresh search. After a great deal of difficulty, during which at one stage he had to remove some of his clothes, Gibbons found Eveline's body in the ash pit, used to collect raw sewage from the water closet. Dr Bushby of Catherine Street was called in to examine the body. After pronouncing life extinct, he had the body removed to the Princes Dock mortuary.

Next morning, at about 8.30 a.m., Robert Parrott, a postman, was crossing the north gate of the Salisbury Dock, when he saw the body of a man lying in a pool of water outside the dock gate, near the sill. The tide was out. With help from a man in charge of a sailing flat, Police Constable Casement managed to retrieve the body. The dead man was John William Bennett, Mrs Murray's missing lodger. His body was identified at the mortuary by his father Henry Bennett, an iron moulder from Lincoln Street in Hull, by Mrs Murray and by David Chapman.

On Saturday 26 January 1901 at Liverpool Coroner's Court, inquests were held into the deaths of both Eveline Christofferson (she was the child of her mother's first husband) and John Bennett. Medical evidence was given by Dr Bushby. He said Eveline had died from bleeding from a knife wound in her throat. She had also been strangled with a scarf and there had been an attempt at violation. Maud Carley, a young woman who had worked for a time for Mrs Murray as a domestic servant, said she remembered, at about the beginning of the previous November, Bennett saying in the kitchen at Parr Street: 'If I can't get work, I will kill someone, and swing for it'. He was out of work then. A few days later, Maud heard Bennett say to Eveline: 'If I was your father, I would murder you'. Maud took no notice of these remarks, thinking them harmless.

The inquest jury brought in a verdict of 'wilful murder' against John William Bennett. As for Bennett's death, Dr Bushby said there were no marks of violence on his body. Death was due to drowning and the jury's verdict on Bennett was 'found drowned'. The coroner said he had visited the scene of the crime. The yard was very small, and the ash pit was intended for use by two houses. He said: 'I cannot understand how such a place is allowed to exist by any landlord anywhere. I hope that some very different arrangement will be made in future with regard to the ash pit. It is disgusting at present and how people are expected to live there I cannot understand'.

Raymond Street

On Monday 18 February 1901 at the Liverpool Assizes in St George's Hall before Mr Justice Bigham, 25-year-old James Maloney was charged with the murder of Margaret Roxburgh.

The dead woman lived with her husband at 65 Raymond Street, off Vauxhall Road. Maloney and his wife lived in the same street. At about 8.00 a.m. on 22 December 1900, Margaret Roxburgh went out to do some shopping. That evening, when she turned up at the house of Maloney's father at 7 Raymond Street, she was very much under the influence of drink. Then James Maloney arrived, also under the influence, as was the elder Maloney and two of Margaret's brothers-in-law, Archie and Jimmy Roxburgh.

A dispute arose between Maloney and his father, about a letter written to the father by one of his sons serving in the Boer War. Margaret said that Maloney himself should have gone to South Africa to fight, instead of marrying a widow with five children. The quarrel intensified. Margaret tried to hit James Maloney with a poker and an ash pan. She left the house with the two Roxburghs, followed soon afterwards by Maloney and his father.

In the street, the dispute continued. Margaret began calling Maloney names. She tried to hit him but was prevented by Mr Maloney senior. Ultimately, she turned to go back into the house. At this, Maloney broke away from his father and, shouting threats, ran after Margaret with a knife in his hand. He followed her into the house.

Old Mr Maloney went after the warring couple. He found them struggling on the floor and he tried to separate them. Eventually, he dragged his son away from the screaming woman. Sarah Nolan, from 55 Raymond Street, hearing screams, went into No. 7, where she found Margaret lying on the kitchen floor, bleeding from a stomach wound. Margaret was taken to the Northern Hospital. It was just after midnight on 23 December. On Christmas Day morning, Margaret Roxburgh died from peritonitis, set up by her wound.

At the hospital, Margaret made a 'dying deposition', a statement on oath, in the presence of Mr Davies, assistant clerk to the city magistrates. She said she had known Maloney for fifteen years. At 11.00 p.m. on the 22nd, when Maloney and his father started to quarrel, she told James not to strike his father. Afterwards, in the street, Maloney saw her and made a rush after her. She ran into No. 7 and shut the door in his face. Later, however, Maloney found his way in and, grabbing hold of her, snarled: 'I've got you now'. Screaming with fear, Margaret shrieked: 'Jimmy, Jimmy, don't kill me!' The father too cried out for help, but the people who came up stood at the door, frightened to venture inside.

Maloney, said Margaret, gave her 'a rip with a penknife'. 'He gave me three prongs, but I cannot say where'. She said she had drunk three glasses of beer and half a glass of brandy between 7.30 p.m. and 11.00 p.m. that night. When he stabbed her, James Maloney said she 'was the worst for drink'.

In defence of Margaret Roxburgh, Mr Madden called no witnesses. Instead, he spoke to the jury. He said: 'The death of the unfortunate woman was brought about as a result of one of those drunken orgies which disgrace Liverpool and other large cities on a Saturday night. It would be idle for even the prosecution to say that the prisoner formed any intent to take the woman's life. There could have been no malice aforethought'. Asking the jury for a verdict of manslaughter, Mr Madden said: 'The provocation the prisoner received from the woman was such as no sober man could withstand. It was altogether too much for a drunken man'.

Addressing the jury, the judge said that no amount of provocation could excuse homicide unless it was of such a character as to deprive the person who committed the crime of all self-control. The fact that the man was drunk and that the crime arose from a drunken row had nothing to do with the case. The man, said the judge, 'was obviously in possession of his senses so as to make him accountable to the law'. The judge said it was manslaughter if Maloney 'did not know practically what he was doing'.

The jury returned a verdict of not guilty of murder, but guilty of manslaughter. After being sentenced by Mr Justice Bigham to fifteen years penal servitude, James Maloney left the dock sobbing bitterly.

A St Helens Poisoning

On Friday 8 March 1901, Mr Brighouse, the Lancashire County Coroner, opened an inquest at St Helens town hall into the death of Jane Simms Johnson, aged 14 months, the only child of Margaret and William Johnson of 72 New Cross Street. Mrs Johnson, who had attempted to commit suicide, was being held in police custody.

The coroner read out the police report, which said that the child, Jane, was in good health until noon on 6 March. Mr Johnson went to his work at 6.45 a.m., leaving his wife Margaret and the child in the house. When Mr Johnson returned at 4.15 p.m. he knocked on the door but got no answer. He went to a neighbour for a key. On opening the door he found his wife lying on a sofa in the kitchen. She looked very ill. He asked her what she had been doing. She said she had taken rat poison. He asked her where Jane was. She told him the child was upstairs in bed, dead. Mr Johnson went up and found that this was indeed true. He called in his neighbour, a Mrs Innes. Mrs Johnson said to her: 'Janey is dead. I will not live. I have taken too much poison. Nobody knew my mind. I was ashamed to go out. I am sorry to have done it, and I shall have to suffer'. She said she had given the child rat poison in warm milk and that she had died in her arms.

Mrs Johnson had appeared at the police court the day before for stealing and pawning a coat belonging to a Mrs Vina Collins of Albion Street. She was bound over under the First Offenders Act. On the way home from court, Mrs Johnson had said to Mrs Collins: 'I will bloody well poison myself and this too', meaning the child in her arms.

The Coroner said that a letter had been found, written in pencil. The envelope was addressed 'To My Husband'. The letter read: 'Dear husband – I cannot bear this any longer. I should certainly have gone off it. I felt I could not rest. I knew you were too good for me. Don't upset yourself in any way. I would have caused you more trouble. I could not bear to look at anyone. I was despised by everybody after the case. I thought it best to take little Janey with me. Everybody knows how good you were to me, so good-bye. Make the best of it. Keep you heart up, for I would have caused more trouble. I have often wished I was dead. When I told Janey she had not long to live, she said, "Me, mama". I loved her but what could I do? I was fast everywhere. Tell my mother not to weep for me because I have been a bad young woman, so goodbye and God guard you for I have been guarded. Kisses from little Janey. Tell my mother not to tell our Alice but give her a kiss from Janey'. After this letter was read out, the inquest was adjourned and re-opened on Monday 25 March.

Several witnesses then gave evidence before the coroner and his jury. Mr Brighouse had Mrs Johnson removed from court so that she would not hear the distressing evidence and 'be the object of idle curiosity'. Mr Johnson said that recently his wife had been getting drunk and into debt. There had been two children who had died from infantile diseases and she was again expecting a child. Then there was the business of Mrs Collins's coat. Mrs Collins said she would have withdrawn the larceny charge had it not been taken out of her hands by the police. She denied she had borne a grudge against Margaret Johnson and then left the witness box in tears.

Charles Swift, a chemist of Baldwin Street, St Helens, described how, on 6 March at about 2.30 p.m., Mrs Johnson came in to his shop and bought a 3*d*. packet of 'vermin killer'. He believed the poison contained strychnine, about 2 grains in each packet. The coroner said that this was enough to kill two people. Medical witnesses said no strychnine had been found in Jane's body, part of a stomach contents sample having been accidentally lost. Death was due to convulsions. Nevertheless, after an absence of half and hour, the jury gave a verdict of 'wilful murder' against Mrs Johnson. Next day, she appeared in the police court in Dale Street and was committed for trial at the assizes.

The trial of Margaret Elizabeth Johnson was held before Mr Justice Wills on Monday 6 May 1901. Mrs Johnson looked extremely weak and ill, supported in the dock by a lady warder. Given a seat, she pleaded 'not guilty' in a low, distressed voice. Outlining the prosecution case, Mr Tobin said: 'The real and substantial question the jury will have to consider is whether, when she killed the child, she was insane in the eyes of the law'. Mr Tobin described how Mrs Johnson had opened her heart to her neighbour, Mrs Ruth Innes: 'Janey is dead. I gave her some rat poison in warm milk. I won't live myself. I have taken too much poison. No one knows my mind. I was ashamed to go out. I bought a night-dress for Janey and I have bought a chemise for myself. The night-gown is to be put on Janey.' To another neighbour who was called in she said: 'I nursed Janey until she was dead. I said to her, "Bless you my child, you have not long to live". If Bill had come home an hour later I should have been dead too. I have gone though the worst. I would rather have died, and I will have to suffer for it now.' On leaving the chemist's shop after buying the poison, she went to Mrs Innes and gave her the house key, saying: 'When Bill comes home hand him the key'.

When Mrs Johnson was committed for trial, she said: 'I am too weak to say much. It all seems a dream to me, but I did hear voices outside the house speaking about me. I don't know what I really gave the child. I know I gave it some milk. I suddenly found my poor child dead in my arms. I knew it was to be. Then I must have fainted away. I had been bad for four or five months like I was before the other two babies. I feel I cannot go

Executions of women who had killed their infant children were rare. They were usually treated with mercy by the courts. The Capital Punishment Commission of 1864–66 found it was established practice to commute the death sentence on women who had murdered their own child (of an age of 12 months or under) to a lesser sentence. Mental disorders occurring after childbirth, usually referred to as puerperal psychosis, were recognised as a reason why a mother could kill her child. The symptoms of this psychosis were delirium, depression, anxiety, catatonia and hallucinations.

Sometimes children were killed for other reasons, such as to conceal an illegitimate birth. In 1861 the Offences against the Person Act made it an offence to conceal the birth of a child by disposing of the body.

through it all again. I hope God will forgive me for wanting to kill myself.' When this was read out, Mrs Johnson wept in the dock, tended by the warder at her side.

Two medical men testified as to Mrs Johnson's state of mind. Dr Price of Walton Prison, who saw her first on 12 March, said she was then in a state of profound depression, weeping, wailing and bemoaning. He recorded that she was suffering from acute melancholia. She accused herself of having stolen something, and said she could not live with the crime. Dr Wriglesworth of Rainhill Asylum said that when he examined Mrs Johnson in April she was insane. He thought that at the time of the crime she was suffering from melancholia, and was not responsible for her actions. Her pregnancy would, he claimed, predispose her to mental disturbance.

The jury decided that Margaret Johnson was 'guilty but insane'. The judge ordered her to be detained at His Majesty's pleasure.

Portland Street

At the assizes on Friday 10 May 1901 Patrick Finnegan, 47, faced a charge of murdering William Carr at Liverpool on 24 March.

Carr was a marine fireman and he and his wife lived in the front bedroom of 106 Portland Street, to the west of Scotland Road. Finnegan and his wife lived in the house which was back to back with No. 106. This was 119 Back Portland Street. No. 106 was also occupied by Patrick Uriel and his wife. The back bedroom was used by one of Uriel's sons.

On the night of the tragedy, Carr got home, stayed in his room for a short while, and then went out through the back door into the yard which separated his house from Finnegan's. His idea, it seems, was to look for his wife, who was Mrs Finnegan's daughter and Finnegan's step-daughter. That night there was some quarrelling and fighting between the two men at No. 119.

At 11.40 p.m. Finnegan went to a policeman stationed in Limekiln Lane and asked him to go to his house. He said Carr had burst open his door and wanted to fight. Finnegan was bleeding from a face wound, which he

Back Portland Street.
Liverpool Record Office, Liverpool Libraries and Information Services

said Carr had inflicted. The policeman went to the house, where he found Carr and Mrs Finnegan. He got Carr to go to his own house and Finnegan went to a dispensary for first aid, arriving there at 12.15 a.m. He had two small cuts on his face. He then went to the detective office and demanded that Carr be arrested. He got home before 1.00 a.m.

By this time, Carr had gone to bed and his house doors were locked. Mary Uriel, the daughter of the tenant of the house, had sat up to wait for her brother, who got home at about 12.45 a.m. She let him in and they sat in the kitchen for a while. They heard someone at the back door so the girl went and asked, 'Who's there?' Finnegan replied, 'It's me'. He was with his wife and the girl let them both in. Finnegan had no boots on and wore only a shirt and trousers. He went straight upstairs into Carr's room while his wife stayed below and talked with Mary Uriel. Mary remembered hearing a match struck, and somebody calling out: 'You cow!' Then Finnegan came back downstairs and left with his wife. Mary locked the door and returned to the kitchen.

Almost immediately, Mary and her brother heard what was later described as 'a snoring or moaning sound from upstairs'. Then there was the sound of somebody getting out of bed. Afraid, they stayed in the kitchen. Mrs Carr, because of her husband's drunken condition, did not go home that night. She slept on a doorstep until 1.20 a.m., when she was wakened by a passing policeman. Mrs Carr then went to Finnegan's house, was let in, and stayed there the night.

At about 5.00 a.m., Mrs Uriel heard a strange snoring sound from the room above her bed. Without going upstairs to investigate, she went to Finnegan's house, knocked and said something was wrong. Mrs Carr came back with her to No. 106. Carr was found on the landing outside his room, practically smothered in blood from a wound to his neck. The clothes on Carr's bed were also covered with blood and a track of blood led across the room. At the Northern Hospital, Carr was pronounced dead on arrival. A stab wound an inch long and 1½ inches deep above his collarbone had severed an artery.

At the police office, Finnegan said: 'I did go upstairs to see if Carr's wife was there'. A knife had been found in a box in Finnegan's room but when it was shown to him, he denied it was his. When charged with murder, Finnegan denied going upstairs and stabbing Carr.

In his words to the jury in defence of Finnegan, Mr Madden said: 'Every assize we have wretched stabbing cases due to the terrible record of the Saturday night's proceedings in the city. If the police had arrested Carr for drunkenness the tragedy might not have occurred. The affair is one of those drunken orgies which all the parties interested are deprived of their reason and are little above the level of brute beasts'. Mr Madden drew the jury's attention to the fact that after the Finnegans had first gone, Carr called out in a strong voice: 'I'll cow you!' He claimed that Finnegan went to Carr's house to look for his daughter and that was his only reason.

The jury were out for ten minutes. The verdict was 'guilty of manslaughter'. The judge, sentencing Finnegan to twenty years penal servitude, said the case was 'as near to murder as a case of manslaughter can be'.

A Case Collapses

On Friday 17 May 1901, Liverpool Deputy Coroner Mr E. Gibson presided over an inquest into the death of 29-year-old Mary McConville. She was believed to have been slain by the man she had lived with for eight years,

Henry Ratcliffe. For the previous year or so, they had been living at 107 Haigh Street, off Islington. Ratcliffe, who was in police custody, was in court when the inquest opened.

The first witness was Arthur McConville, Mary's brother, who lived in the same house. On Tuesday morning, 14 May, Ratcliffe left the house at about 10.30 a.m. while Arthur stayed in the house with his sister. At about 12.30 p.m. a woman called Annie Denham came in with two gills of beer. That afternoon, she and the two McConvilles drank, according to Arthur, 'about eight gills'. At 3.30 p.m., Annie Denham and Mary McConville went out drinking until 7.30 p.m. Arthur sent out for more drink and they had, he said, 'four gills'.

Arthur recalled how Ratcliffe and some other men arrived at the house. Mary was sitting on the sofa by the window and Ratcliffe stood by the fire. They started to argue about something. According to McConville, Ratcliffe knocked his sister to the floor by hitting her in the face three or four times. After going back to the fireplace for a moment, Ratcliffe went over to the

Drink

In several of these cases alcohol, both in the form of beer and spirits, was sent out for. Drunkenness was a social problem in many cities around the country and was one of the means of escape from the daily grind and poverty. In the years 1908–9 62,882 people were sent to jail for drunkenness. The true levels of drunkenness, however, were likely to have been higher as the police would have been unable to arrest and charge everybody they found drunk in the street; they would resort to moving a person on, unless they became disorderly making arrest inevitable. Drunkenness in the home, of course, was hidden from the street and the authorities. Public houses were attractive as they were warm and convivial and there were plenty of them in Liverpool. Until 1915 public houses could open from 5 a.m. to 12.30 p.m. The need for a sober workforce, particularly in munitions factories, was the reason for restrictions imposed through the licensing laws; before this both brewing companies and drinkers resisted any attempt to restrict hours or the number of licensed premises.

fallen woman and 'kicked her three or four times about the lower part of her body'. When Arthur interfered, Ratcliffe said to him: 'You're not going to boss this house'. Then he hit McConville on the jaw. A struggle broke out between the two men as the other men fled outside. Ratcliffe wanted McConville to go into the street and fight it out but McConville refused. Ratcliffe then walked away from the scene.

Arthur McConville said that when he went back into the house, he found his sister sitting on the sofa. She asked him to get her a bucket. He got her one and helped her to sit on it. Releasing his hold on her for a moment to get his pipe, she fell and fainted. There was blood on the floor beneath her. Mary told him she had been kicked in her womb. He put her on to the sofa again. Arthur then went down William Henry Street to look for a policeman. On his return, he found his sister lying on the kitchen floor. Two women were with her. They told him she was dead.

The second witness was Annie Denham. She said she saw Ratcliffe knock Mary down but had no more distinct recollection of any further events. In fact, it was only Arthur McConville who remembered seeing Ratcliffe kick Mary. Other witnesses said they saw no kick. Margaret Worrall, a neighbour, remembered meeting Annie Denham in Haigh Street. Denham shouted out to her: 'Arthur had knocked her off the sofa and then kicked her'. Recalled to the witness box, Annie Denham said she did not remember seeing Mrs Worrall, but she did say to someone: 'Mary is dying on the hearthstone'. It was Harry Ratcliffe who hit and kicked his wife, not Arthur. The witness heard Denham say: 'Poor Mary's brother has done it'.

When taken by the police, Ratcliffe said he knew nothing about his partner's death. When Constable Roby arrived at the house, Arthur McConville pointed to Ratcliffe, who sat in a corner, and said: 'That fellow did it. He struck her on the sofa and then kicked her'. Dr Jones from the East Dispensary arrived at 9.30 p.m. but Mary was already dead from a wound in the abdomen.

The inquest jury returned a verdict of 'wilful murder' against Ratcliffe. As he left the court, he waved to a female witness and said: 'Ta, ta'. Next day he was ordered to face trial for murder at the assizes.

Harry Ratcliffe's case came up before Mr Justice Ridley at St George's Hall on Friday 2 August 1901. Dr Evans, who carried out the post mortem examination, said that the woman's death had been caused by her being kicked. The judge said there was 'no positive evidence as to who

One of the duties of a Coroner's jury was to ascertain whether a person or persons should be charged with murder, manslaughter, infanticide or as an accessory to murder. The Broderick Committee in 1976 recommended that the power of a Coroner to commit a person to trial be ended, although the practice went on until as late as 1978.

administered the kick'. Because the prosecution had to rely on the evidence of Arthur McConville, uncorroborated by any other witness, he directed that Ratcliffe be acquitted. The jury foreman then gave a formal verdict of 'not guilty'. Harry Ratcliffe went free without punishment.

Adelaide Place

On Thursday 11 July 1901, 24-year-old Annie Turner appeared before stipendiary magistrate W. J. Stewart charged with the wilful murder of Luke Crean, 28, a coal heaver of 11 Dryden Street. The killing took place during a street row in Adelaide Place, Roscommon Street, on the night of Monday 8 July. Crean was said to have been hit on the head with a hatchet. He died from a fractured skull in the Northern Hospital. Annie Turner was remanded in custody by the magistrate.

Next day, the inquest on Crean opened at the coroner's court. It was quickly adjourned and resumed the following Wednesday. By now, in addition to Annie Turner's murder charge, four men were in custody in connection with the Adelaide Place disturbance.

The first witness at the inquest was Pierce Lacy, a coal heaver of Adelaide Place. He said that on the afternoon of 8 July, when he got home, he found in his house Luke Crean, his brother Patrick Crean, William Brew, Thomas Maloney, and two men called Carr and Singleton. They were all the worse for drink and were intent on drinking more. Carr went out at about 3.30 p.m. Coming back a few minutes later, Carr said he had been insulted by some men outside in the street. A few moments after Carr's arrival, the door was burst open and three or four men, standing outside, challenged the others to come out and fight, saying: 'Send out the best man in the house'. Like Crean, Brew, Maloney and Singleton went out. Lacy said he thought two of the challenging men were the Jenkins brothers, but he was not certain of this. Lacy stayed in the house with the others. He said he saw nothing of the fight which ensued in the street.

Mary Holland, who lived in a court off Great Homer Street, said she saw six men fighting in Adelaide Place. Annie Turner was standing in the street, tapping her chest and shouting: 'True Blue and No surrender'. She joined in the fight for a while and then went in to the house. Annie came out with a hatchet in her left hand and then hit Luke Crean twice on the head with the blunt part of the hatchet. The first blow was heavy, the second one lighter. A cry of 'Police!' was raised, upon which Luke Crean and two other men fell into a cellar.

Sarah Flanagan, of 12 Court, Great Homer Street, said she saw Luke Crean and two other men fighting together, surrounded by a big crowd. She saw Annie Turner strike Crean once on the left side of his head with the flat part of the hatchet. She told Annie she was wrong to do such a thing and Annie replied: 'Well, they are all on to our Emma'. Luke Crean was brought out of the cellar by a policeman but he escaped and ran away.

Annie Turner was identified to the police by a woman called Margaret McCabe of 18 Creer Street. After the fight, Annie took Margaret to a pub and bought her some drinks. Annie said: 'I hit a man with a hatchet, and if he comes back I'll do the same to him.' It was the season of religious marches and referring to this, the coroner said: 'It is an unfortunate time of year'. Mr Quilliam, acting for Annie Turner, replied: 'You know what the poet says: "They kill each other for the love of God".'

Another eyewitness to the affray was Florence Rushworh of 70 Vergil Street. She said she saw Luke Crean fighting with Thomas Henry Jenkins. Mr Jenkins stepped between the two men and pushed them apart. Crean fell over and Mrs Jenkins hit him about a dozen times with the heel of a slipper. Then Annie Turner brought out the hatchet and hit Crean on the head. He put his hand to his head and called out: 'Now you have done it!' Annie took the hatchet into the house. As she put it away in a corner she said: 'I have helped to kill one Orangeman, and I will kill another'. Bleeding from his head and left ear, Crean was taken by the police to hospital, where he died. The inquest jury's verdict was 'wilful murder' against Annie Turner.

Annie Rachael Turner stood trial at the assizes before Mr Justice Ridley and a jury on Thursday 1 August 1901. It seems that in the neighbourhood of Adelaide Place there were two rival religious factions, amongst whom there was a lot of drunkenness and general lawlessness. Luke Crean and other coal heavers had been to Canada Dock but had failed to find any work. They had then done the round of various pubs before arriving in Adelaide Place.

The twelve-man trial jury found Annie Turner guilty of manslaughter. The justice issued her with a sentence of fifteen years penal servitude.

Sectarianism

From the late Victorian period right through to the beginning of World War Two, Liverpool was greatly affected by sectarian divisions and violence. The problems within the city were comparable with Belfast and Glasgow.

Irish migration into Liverpool increased dramatically in the 1840s as a result of the Potato Famine in Ireland. Liverpool was quite literally the gateway to the world, and many different peoples passed through it to America, Canada, Australia and New Zealand. Not all could afford the cost of passage overseas, however, and many Irish settled in Liverpool. The city gained a large Irish Catholic presence which would eventually begin to clash with English and Northern Irish Protestants who had also made their way to the city. Catholics and Protestants settled in different areas – for example, Scotland Road was predominantly Catholic while Netherfield Road area was populated by Protestants. This segregation did nothing to reduce the level of mistrust and suspicion between the two communities. This was made worse by the exploitation by local politicians and tub-thumping preachers, such as Pastor George Wise.

The religious divide also coloured the city's politics. Several leading members of the Conservative Party in Liverpool were also members of the Orange Lodge and there were several Irish

Nationalists sitting on the city council. Home Rule for Ireland was a high-profile issue during the years up to the First World War and the debates and tensions involving this issue, and fear of Catholicism, Popery and the power of priests, spilled over on to the streets of Liverpool in periodic outbreaks of violence and mayhem.

The main days for trouble between the two communities were naturally 17 March, St Patrick's Day, and 12 July, the anniversary of the Battle of the Boyne. Pat O'Mara, born in 1901, vividly describes the divisions and violence in his *Autobiography of a Liverpool Slummy*:

'A huge crowd of our worst enemies (the "Os") with bands and banners carrying inscriptions that made our blood boil, surged around us. Orange everywhere and not a bit of green! I had never known there were so many enthusiastic Protestants. I had always been brought up in the belief that Protestantism was a dying cult, and its adherents cowards, easily frightened; but this mob up here, led by that magnificent white horse bearing a little boy dressed as a perfect duplicate of Prince William, didn't look frightened at all.'

This march steered clear of Catholic areas, but one march O'Mara recounted strayed past St Francis Catholic Church in Shaw Street, where three priests were being ordained:

'The flaunting Protestant banners drew alongside the church at the very moment when the Catholic crowd surged out of it. Bedlam was the result. The little child who impersonated King Billy on his white charger had his head staved in with a brick, falling off the horse bleeding and screaming with pain.'

Child Starvation at Birkenhead

In August 1901 an inquest jury at Birkenhead heard of the tragic death of a five-month-old girl called Mary Jane Mahon, the illegitimate daughter of a 21-year-old woman called Jane Mahon who was living in Orderly Avenue in the town. Borough Coroner Cecil Holden presided.

The child's mother and the grandmother, Annie Mahon, 62, had already been arrested and had appeared before the magistrates on a charge of manslaughter. The mother had said to Detective Chief Inspector Parker that she was out working every day, and left the baby with the grandmother. She said a doctor had attended the baby and had prescribed medicine, but the grandmother, she said, threw it away. Annie Mahon had told Parker that the child had been too weak to take food and medicine and had suffered a great deal from convulsions. Poignant photographs of the child in life and in death showed she was almost a skeleton.

In evidence, Dr Sydney Wilkinson described how, the previous March, he had been called to the Mahons' house in Orderly Avenue. On arrival, he found Jane Mahon in the process of giving birth to a healthy baby girl. The house was in a miserable state and there was no food in the place. The doctor informed the parish relieving officer and advised that the younger woman be removed to the workhouse. Jane Mahon had been working since June at a laundry for a Mrs Warburton for two shillings a day.

Agnes Meney, who lived at 6 Orderly Avenue, next door to the Mahons, spoke to the court about their drunken habits and of another daughter, a Mrs Mulholland, who also lived there and had three children of her own. Jane had a second child aged 2½ years. Annie Mahon was supposed to look after the children in the daytime but, said Mrs Meney, she was 'of dirty and drunken habits'. As evidence of starvation, Mrs Meney said she saw 'only three separate halfporths of milk go into the house during several weeks'. She saw the old woman giving the child 'a halfp'orth of milk mixed with nearly half a pint of water'. She complained about this to Annie Mahon but was told to mind her own business. The house, she said, was filthy and the baby's cradle in a shocking state.

The child was taken on 22 August to Dr Wilson at 98 Grange Road. She was, said the doctor, 'in a filthy, neglected and emaciated condition'. He reported the matter to inspector Hallett of the Society for Prevention of Cruelty to Children. Hallett found the child 'filthy and covered with vermin, terribly emaciated'. She weighed only 5½ pounds. There was a ginger beer bottle with a rubber tube, from which the mother fed condensed milk. Living in the room was Annie Mahon, Mrs Mulholland, Jane and the five children. After being admitted to the children's shelter on 23 August, the child died on the 28th.

Called in at the death of the child, Dr Dalzell of Hamilton Square had found her in an old box in a corner of the room at Orderly Avenue, with filthy bedding. She was skin and bone from long neglect. The pectoral and abdominal muscles had atrophied and had almost disappeared. Death was due to exhaustion owing to starvation.

Little Mary Jane's father was a man called James McCann who was living at 353 Brook Street. In court he said that the marriage banns were put up at St Mary's church when he was in prison. The only money he had contributed to Jane Mahon was 'what she stole from me when I was drunk'.

When she was charged with causing the death of her child, Jane said: 'How could I cause it when I was out working all day? My mother had the care of the child. I got medicine from Dr Wilson and my mother threw it away'. When charged, the grandmother, Annie Mahon said: 'I could not help God's will. She would not drink milk or take the breast. She cried all night and was in convulsions.'

The inquest jury's verdict was 'wilful murder' against Annie and Jane Mahon. On Tuesday 3 September, the two women were committed on bail to stand trial for manslaughter. At Chester Assizes on Tuesday 5 November, a trial jury found both women guilty of the manslaughter of little Mary Jane. After postponing sentence for a day, Mr Justice Phillimore gave Annie nine months imprisonment. Jane Mahon, who promised to enter the home of the Convent of the Good Shepherd at Fulham and remain there for a year, was bound over in the sum of twenty pounds.

Baptist Street

After receiving a message from the governor of the Liverpool Workhouse on Brownlow Hill, Detective Chief Inspector Robertson visited the workhouse at 11.30 p.m. on Friday 11 October 1901. He took down a statement made by one of the patients, Catherine McAllister, 32, of Baptist Street. The statement read: 'I am the wife of Thomas McAllister and live at 42 Baptist Street, Liverpool. I was brought here yesterday. I am suffering from a stab in the back. I believe I am dying, and do not expect to get better. I was stabbed in Christian Street at the bottom of Springfield Street. It was about 11.00 p.m. on Monday last. My husband done it. It was all through jealousy. He had no cause to be jealous. He was drunk. He came up to me and got hold of me, and got the knife and stuck me in the back. His mother took me to her house. I was afterwards taken home, and he washed my wound and put some plasters on it'. Catherine McAllister's words were uttered with long pauses, lasting sometimes for five minutes. Realising that the woman's formal deposition should be taken, Robertson contacted Major Hewitt JP and Mr Davies, the magistrate's clerk. However, by the time they arrived at the hospital, Mrs McAllister was dead.

An inquest was held on 22 October 1901. Ellen Timlin, who lodged at 42 Baptist Street, told the court that Catherine McAllister was 'a hard working steady woman'. Her husband Thomas 'has a hot temper and is given to drink'. About six weeks earlier he had returned home after an absence of three years. He told Ellen he had been doing penal servitude for 'cutting' his wife. He was often much the worse for drink, and frequently ill-treated Catherine. Three weeks previously, Ellen heard McAllister say that he 'would be the death of her' and that he would as soon be in prison as out of it. Ellen Timlin then described how, at about 1 a.m. on 8 October, when she was in bed, McAllister rushed into her bedroom. He said he 'had killed one and would kill two'. He kicked Ellen several times and hit her with his fist. She asked him what was the matter. McAllister said: 'I have stabbed my wife and broken the knife I done it with'.

Sergeant Kelly arrested Thomas McAllister and charged him with murder. He replied: 'I am as innocent as a child. She went out on Wednesday to separate a fight, and when she came back she complained of a pain underneath the breast.'

Dr Martin, a resident surgeon at the Workhouse Hospital, said Catherine McAllister was admitted on the evening of 10 October. She told him she had been separating a man and wife fighting in Christian Street, and had got a small stab in the back. The knife, said Dr Martin, had penetrated her left lung. Death was due to haemorrhage caused by the wound.

At the end of the evidence, deputy coroner E. A. Gibson said: 'There is no evidence of any provocation or anything to justify a manslaughter verdict'. As expected, the jury's verdict was 'wilful murder'.

McAllister's murder trial was held at St George's Hall before Mr Justice Bucknill. The prosecution case was that Catherine and her mother left the house at Baptist Street, followed soon afterwards by Thomas McAllister. He went up behind his wife and stabbed her. It was near the junction of Christian Street and Springfield Street. Within two hours of the stabbing, McAllister admitted he was responsible, while Catherine herself said she had been stabbed when separating a fight.

At the trial, Ellen Timlin described how, after the stabbing, she was with the McAllister couple. Thomas said: 'I am sorry now for what I have done'. Catherine said: 'I am very bad, Tommy', to which he replied: 'As soon as we get a cup of tea I will see what's the matter with you'. They went upstairs together. When Thomas came down he said: 'It's only the scratch of a pin'.

After consulting together for 1½ hours, the jury brought in a verdict of 'guilty of manslaughter'. McAllister pleaded for mercy 'for the sake of my poor old mother and two orphaned sisters. The shock will kill her.' But he had a very bad record, having served three years already for wounding his wife, and the judge said: 'The poor wife has been a sober woman, the prisoner a drunken blackguard. The jury has taken a merciful view of the case but no one can feel any sympathy for such a worthless, drunken fellow'. The sentence was fifteen years penal servitude.

Rose Cottage

St George's Hall was the scene for the 'trial of the year' on Monday 2 December 1901 and crowds queued up early to ensure seats in the public gallery. The accused was John Harrison, 31, charged with murdering Alice Ann Wright on 27 July 1901. The judge was Mr Justice Bucknill. Mr Ford led for the prosecution and Mr Greer for the defence.

Mr Ford said that Harrison had committed 'a very barbarous and

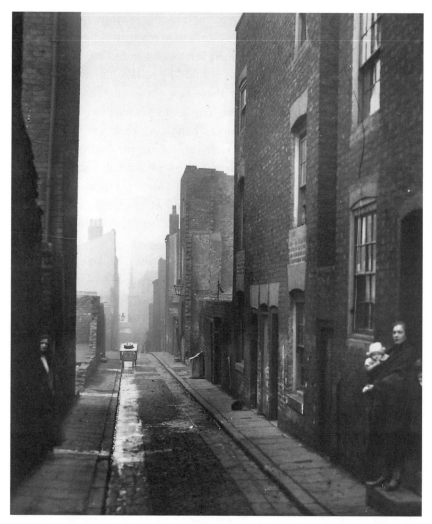

Baptist Street.
Liverpool Record Office, Liverpool Libraries and Information Services

premeditated murder', indicating immediately that he considered manslaughter out of the question. Harrison and Alice Wright had gone through a marriage ceremony at Parr in February 1901 but Alice already had a husband. They were living together at Ormskirk. On 26 July, the day before the tragedy, the couple made enquiries about a cottage to let at Bickerstaffe near Rainford. On the 27th, they arrived at the cottage at about 10 a.m. It was called Rose Cottage and was in a very lonely spot, surrounded by farmland, about two hundred yards from Rose Farm. It had three rooms. To the left side of the kitchen was an alcove, where Alice Wright's body was found.

Peter Marsh of Rose Farm owned Rose Cottage and on 27 July, Alice Wright called on him and said she would like to take the cottage. Marsh went with her to the cottage and there saw Harrison, who said he had been working at Rainford Colliery. He let the cottage to them, unfurnished. When Marsh left the couple at the cottage it was 9.45 a.m. At 9.00 p.m. that night, Marsh met Harrison again, who told him: 'My wife is dead'. 'What?' asked Marsh. 'My wife is dead and cold', said Harrison. 'I went to St Helens and my wife went to Skem, and now that I come back I find her on the floor dead and cold.' Marsh advised Harrison to go for a policeman. He walked with him a short while to show him the way.

Rachael Thompson, 15, of Ivy Farm, passed Rose Cottage at 1.20 p.m. on the 27th. She was on her way back from a dressmaking lesson in Skelmersdale. She noticed that the cottage window was broken, the glass lying on the footpath. Rachael went round to the back and looked into the two back rooms. She then came back to the front door and opened it. She saw a white straw hat and a garment covering someone lying on the floor. Thinking she saw a drunken man lying asleep, she closed the door and went home. She had actually seen the body of Alice Wright.

At 1.10 p.m. that day, William Evans came across John Harrison near the footpath which led to Rose Cottage. He was hurrying away from the path with his head down, going towards White Moss Colliery.

Harrison had made several contradictory statements about finding his wife. Mrs Wragg, wife of the police constable at Bickerstaffe, related how, at about 9.30 p.m., Harrison came to her house asking for a policeman. She said her husband was out but would be back soon. Mrs Wragg asked Harrison what he wanted him for. He said: 'I have found my wife dead on the ground'. To this, Mrs Wragg said: 'That's funny, is it not? There must have been something ailing her'. Harrison replied: 'She seemed as though somebody had been meddling with her throat'. To Miles Cunliffe, a policeman stationed at Skelmersdale, Harrison said he had found his wife dead, but that he had not stopped to examine her. He was drunk at the time he spoke to Cunliffe. Harrison told Sergeant Kidd that he had left the house at 12.00 p.m. to go to his work at Rainford Siding and he returned to the cottage at 9.00 p.m.

The straw hat was laid on the woman's head and its hatpin had no hold on the hair. There was blood on Alice's bodice, and the distinct impression of a woman's left hand in the dust on a windowpane (the window was produced in court and examined by the jury). Blood had flowed from a cut on Alice's hand so she had evidently been cut in pushing through the window. Death was due to strangulation. The prosecution believed she was killed in the centre of the kitchen and moved to her final position. Alice had been the purse bearer in their money transactions but not a farthing was found on her. The purse was found on Harrison. There was blood on his thumb and on the wrists of his shirt.

It was clear that Harrison and Alice Wright had been falling out with each other on the day she died. Richard Gardener, a teamster, saw the couple in Skelmersdale on the morning of the 27th. They were walking in the direction of the Engine Hotel, cursing one another. Harrison went into the hotel, closely followed by Alice. Robert Aspinall, a carter on a nearby farm, said he also saw the couple that day. He saw Harrison strike Alice with his fist but, he said: 'I didn't think much about it'.

When Sergeant Kidd charged Harrison with murdering his wife, he said: 'Killing my wife? I would not touch a hair of her head'. In his final words to the jury, defence counsel Mr Greer, who called no witnesses on Harrison's behalf, dealt with what he called 'lack of premeditation'. Mr Greer said: 'These were rough people who were used to hitting each other. They were on good terms when they left the pub.' Mr Greer contended that the facts did not point to premeditation but this was not his defence. His defence was that Harrison was not there, that someone else killed Alice. He explained the blood on Harrison's clothes as coming when he brushed against the dead body while he was examining it.

As was the practice in 1901, court cases were usually continued to a late hour. After the judge had given his summing up, it was 7.55 p.m. when the jury left to consider their verdict. They returned at 9.15 p.m. The foreman announced the verdict: 'Guilty of murder'. Mr Justice Bucknill put on the black cap and pronounced sentence of death. Harrison cried out: 'I am not guilty, sir!' After the words 'may God have mercy on your soul', Harrison said: 'Will he have mercy on us then?'

In the death cell at Walton Prison the condemned man at first appeared callous and frivolous. He asked for a better pair of trousers because those he was wearing were frayed in the legs and were tripping him. The *Daily Post* for Monday 9 December contained the following pen picture of Harrison:

> He eats well, talks, chatters and expresses and opinion about everything. He is annoyed at the price of the execution, thinking the hangman gets too much for his services. He should get £1 and not £5. He goes out twice a day to the exercise ground accompanied by two warders and can then smoke as much as he likes. He is a heavy smoker so longs for this relaxation. He is so anxious to get his pipe lighted. He went to church twice on Sunday and goes during the week, receives the Rev. Morris, the protestant chaplain, with alacrity. He seems indifferent to his fate.

On Saturday 21 December, a petition for a reprieve for Harrison was turned down by the Home Secretary. Harrison's solicitor J. C. Eccles received a short letter which contained a well-used phrase: 'The Home Secretary has failed to discover any sufficient grounds to justify him in advising His

Majesty to interfere with the due course of the law.' Anyone, throughout the period during which capital punishment was applicable, found guilty of murder, was automatically sentenced to death.

The execution was fixed for Christmas Eve. As the fateful day drew nearer, Harrison became humbler and more penitent. On Sunday 22nd, he requested *Lead Kindly Light* be sung in church and that Kebel's hymn *Sun of my Soul* be read to him, then he broke down utterly, saying he was sorry he had ever done anything wrong. In the afternoon of the 23rd, Harrison had a final meeting with his brother Joseph and his sister.

On the Monday evening, hangman William Billington with his assistant, his brother Thomas, arrived at Walton Prison. This was to be Billington's first hanging after being appointed public executioner in succession to his father. During the afternoon a knot of spectators, in spite of the bitter cold, hung about Walton Junction bridge in the hope of satisfying their curiosity. Billington found it no easy task to get along the slippery road, the fierce cutting wind driving him backwards. Special prayers were said for Harrison at St Peter's church in Parr on Sunday. All of those who knew him were quite certain that at various times, and for long periods, he was not right in his head.

On Christmas Eve morning at about 7.30 a.m., people began to assemble in groups, eager to witness the hoisting of the black flag, denoting that the execution had taken place. The weather was cold and rainy. The light did not begin to break over the turrets of the prison until about 7.20 a.m., when the portals of the building gradually loomed up out of the darkness. Warders came and went. Milk carts arrived and delivered their quantities at the prison gates, followed by the officials who were to be present at the

The Capital Punishment Amendment Act 1868 abolished the death sentence for all crimes except murder, treason, piracy and arson in the Royal Dockyards. Murder was the most common offence to lead to the death sentence and to execution. Public executions also ended in this year. These had been a great public spectacle, attracting thousands of people, though the crowds had become more and more disorderly over the years, viewing the executions as entertainment rather than a dire warning for wrongdoing.

The development of the 'long drop' method of hanging, first used in Ireland and then developed in the 1870s by William Marwood, brought to an end the old method of hanging, which effectively meant slow strangulation by which the victims took several agonising minutes to die. Black curtains were hung around the bottom of the scaffold to cover the sight of the prisoner thrashing and twitching as they died. The body would be left to hang for an hour after execution to ensure that the person was dead and to prevent the possibility of him or her being buried alive. This procedure continued even after the old method of hanging had ended. The long drop method made death instantaneous by breaking the neck. Calculations based on a prisoner's weight and height had to be carefully made to produce the correct length of drop. Miscalculation could lead to horrifying results such as decapitation, but on the whole hanging became quick, efficient and unlikely to go wrong. This is given as one of the reasons why after 1875 a greater number of executions were sanctioned.

execution. A few men who had been released early in the morning struggled away towards town, calling first at the temperance shed close to the prison for much needed refreshments. Very shortly before eight the horrid clang of the loud passing bell was heard, indicating that Harrison had been placed in the pinioning room. He had to march out into the courtyard before he reached the execution room, where he had his last glimpse of daylight. He walked firmly and determinedly to the scaffold. Before the white cap was pulled over his face, Harrison admitted his guilt, and said he accepted his punishment as payment for his crime. His last words were, 'Drink, drink, drink!', to which he attributed his downfall. A drop of 6 ft 1 in was used. Death was instantaneous. The body was left hanging for an hour, then placed in a coffin for the examination of the inquest jury, before being buried in quicklime within the prison walls.

❧ 1902 ❦

Beatrice Street, Bootle

On Wednesday 9 April 1902 at Bootle, Samuel Brighouse, the county coroner, opened an inquest into the death of 27-year-old Thomas Sharkey, who was killed at 13 Beatrice Street on 2 April. In custody was James Deeney, 27, who sat in the dock in the police court building.

Patrick Sharkey, brother of the dead man, was the first witness at the inquest. He was a timekeeper at the Lambeth Road tramways depot. Thomas Sharkey had worked as a tram conductor and both brothers lodged with Mrs Mary Finnegan at 13 Beatrice Street. James Deeney was a tram guard who also lodged there. Deeney and the Sharkey brothers slept in the front bedroom, where Deeney had a bed facing the door, while the Sharkeys slept in the bed on the outside when entering the room. Thomas used to sleep on the outside of the bed and Patrick next to the wall.

On Tuesday 1 April Patrick arrived home at 11.00 p.m. Deeney and Thomas were in their beds, and Patrick went to bed at 11.15 p.m. Both of the other men seemed to be asleep so Patrick said nothing to them. He got up next morning at about 3.30 a.m., went out, and returned at about 5.00 a.m. He waited at the front door for about a minute, thinking that his brother would be getting up. Then Patrick heard a noise from inside, like the crash of splintering furniture. He heard his brother cry out, 'Oh, Deeney!' He knocked hard on the door and tried to push it in, but could not. Patrick then ran to the bottom of Beatrice Street to the Stanley Road corner to try to get a policeman.

When Patrick Sharkey got back to the house the door was open and Mrs Malmberg from No. 11 was standing in the doorway. She told him not to go upstairs, which he did anyway, and entered the front room. There was his brother Thomas lying on his back on the floor in a pool of blood. Deeney was in the room, as was a man called Hitman who lodged with Mrs Malmberg. Patrick ran nearby for Dr Powell but when the doctor arrived Thomas Sharkey was, as everyone feared, already dead.

The landlady at 13 Beatrice Street, widow Mary Finnegan, told her story to the coroner and to the inquest jury. She said that on 1 April, Deeney went to bed at about 10.00 p.m., before Thomas Sharkey. He followed a little later. Also living in the house were Mary's two daughters, Charlotte and Louisa. She and the girls were the last to go to bed. Next morning Mary got up at about 5.00 a.m. and heard a noise like someone jumping out of bed on to the floor, following by crockery breaking. Mary next heard Thomas Sharkey shout out, 'Oh, Deeney! Oh, Deeney!' and then a great scream, then a few moans, followed by several thuds. She opened her window to shout for help, but then ran out into the street, not re-entering the house until Dr Powell had arrived.

Produced in court was a fender, very much twisted, dented and damaged. It was from the men's bedroom. Mary Finnegan also identified a chair with two broken spindles. Until about twelve weeks earlier, Deeney had been engaged to Charlotte, as had Thomas Sharkey some three years before that. Deeney had seemingly called off the engagement. Towards the end of March, Deeney had become very moody and restless. He was very upset about a mistake he had made over a tram ticket. Deeney told Mary he had a lawsuit pending and that he believed detectives were watching him. Deeney told her he intended to stay with his relatives in Ireland. He had gone down to the Derry boat that morning, but he saw three detectives watching there so he did not sail on the boat.

The man who was closest to events in the men's bedroom that morning was next door neighbour Wopke Hitman. Wakened by Mrs Malmberg, he hurriedly got dressed, went to the door of No. 13 and kicked it open. Hitman went upstairs, his landlady following. He could hear a noise like someone kicking an empty drum about. The front bedroom door was slightly ajar. In the room Thomas Sharkey was lying on the floor. Deeney was standing at his feet with a fender in his hands. Sharkey lay slightly on his left side. Hitman said: 'Deeney, what are you doing?' Deeney looked over his right shoulder and, remaining silent, dropped the fender. He was trembling with excitement and emotion. Hitman took hold of Deeney by the arm and pushed him on to the bed, where he sat down. Hitman stayed with Deeney until the police arrived. When Deeney had quietened down, Hitman said to him: 'Deeney, my poor lad, what made you do it?' His only reply was 'Ah, Mr Hitman!' When the police officer, Constable Ruxton, asked Deeney 'How did this happen?', Deeney pointed to the foot of the bed, where Hitman stood, and said: 'That beg man told me to fire, and I fired.' A small lighted candle stood on the mantelpiece as dawn began to break.

Just before noon, at the police court building, the inquest jury went into a side room. Five minutes later they gave a verdict of 'wilful murder' against James Deeney.

Deeney's trial was held at the Liverpool Spring Assizes on Tuesday 6 May 1902. After Mr Tobin had questioned the prosecution witnesses, Dr Wriglesworth, medical superintendent at Rainhill Asylum, was called by the defence to give his opinion on Deeney's mental condition. The doctor said he saw Deeney in Walton Gaol on 25 April. Deeney was 'rather moody and in a depressed state'. He was, said the doctor, still suffering from melancholia. He was suffering the delusion that Liverpool Corporation were going to prosecute him for being wrong in his cash. In fact, the cash was absolutely all right. Dr Wriglesworth said he believed Deeney was insane at the time of the murder, the act being done 'in a state of frenzy'. Deeney would not understand the nature of his act. Both his parents had been insane. Deeney was found to be 'guilty but insane' and detained in prison 'until His Majesty's pleasure be known'.

Murder or Suicide at Ashton Street?

The inquest on the body of Ann Elizabeth Walker, 40, of 41 Ashton Street, opened at the Dale Street coroner's court on Thursday 24 April 1902. The husband, James Walker, 50, a sailor, had been arrested and charged with causing her death. After hearing evidence, the inquest jury returned a verdict of 'wilful murder' against Walker, but the jury added that the killing was done 'under great provocation'. Walker's trial opened at the assizes on Monday 5 May before Mr Justice Walton.

Outlining the case against the accused, Mr Ford said that up to the end of February the Walker couple had been living apart in lodgings. It was arranged that the wife should lodge with a Mrs Brown at 41 Ashton Street, occupying the front parlour as a living and sleeping room. The husband returned home from a voyage on 10 April. On 16 April Ann Walker started drinking early in the day. She sent out for some rum and James Walker complained. At 9.30 a.m. he left to go to his work at the docks. Shortly afterwards, Ann went out and did not return until 12.30 p.m. She had called on her 14-year-old daughter Sarah who lived in a children's home in Bootle. She got home drunk. James got in at about 3.00 p.m., slightly under the influence.

The couple began to quarrel. Other people in the house heard a good deal of scuffling. The disturbance increased to such an extent that one of the lodgers, a Mrs Godfrey, had to go to the Walkers' door and ask them to desist. From the heated conversation that was overheard, it appeared that Mrs Walker had pawned some clothes which her husband wanted to wear to go down to his ship.

The woman was heard to cry 'Don't!' followed by a loud scream from her. Then there was a pause, and a minute later another scream, her last. Mrs Godfrey tried to open the door but Walker was pressing heavily against it from the inside. Soon afterwards, Walker came out into the passage. There was blood on his hands. When asked what had happened, he said: 'Go in and look for yourself; she has cut her throat.' Ann Walker was lying in a pool of blood with a large wound in her throat. She died soon afterwards.

Did Ann Walker kill herself? Ann's daughter Sarah said that her mother was addicted to drink and that when she lived with her two years before in South Chester Street, she put a razor across her throat when she was drunk. Sarah said she had never seen her father drunk, nor had she ever seen him threaten to kill her mother. They did have frequent quarrels and her father used to hit her mother. When drunk, her mother had several times threatened to kill herself.

Mrs Brown tried to get the Walkers to live together at Ashton Street. James had told her she had 'sold or pawned two homes' to pay for drink. He said he would pay for her lodgings when he was away at sea. On 9 April Ann Walker expected her husband to come home. He had, however, met with an accident. She seemed troubled about this and knocked her head against the wall in frustration. She also threatened to poison herself. Mrs Brown tried to pacify her, but again Mrs Walker threatened to take her own life. Mrs Brown testified that Mr Walker had tried his best to reform his wife. He had had a great deal of trouble with her, and had forgiven her several times for her bad conduct.

James Walker told several people that his wife had 'done it herself'. However, Dr Wilson, house surgeon at the Royal Infirmary, said Mrs Walker died 25 minutes after being admitted. On examining the wound on the right side of her throat, he found in the neck a piece of blade, broken off the razor which caused the wound. Dr Wilson believed the wound was inflicted by another person, because it needed considerable force. There were several other injuries on the body. Questioned by defence counsel Mr Quilliam, Dr Wilson said the wound could possibly have been self-inflicted. Mr Paul, a surgeon, backed up Dr Wilson's view. He said: 'I feel morally certain it was not a self-inflicted wound. It required considerable violence. It was a typical homicidal wound.' In reply to Mr Quilliam, Mr Paul said it was possible for the woman to have done it herself, but it was not likely. It was doubtful that a right-handed person like Mrs Walker would bring the blade of a razor down the right side of her neck. It was more probable that the weapon would be drawn across the throat from left to right.

James Walker gave evidence in his own defence, questioned by Mr Le Mesurier. He said he had been married to Ann for twenty years. His married life had been very miserable because of his wife's drunken habits. As soon as she got money she would drink it. Several times when he got back from a voyage he found she had cleared his house. He had left her four times, but had later forgiven her. She had many times threatened to take her life and he had taken knives from her. According to Walker, she used her left hand as well as she did her right.

On the afternoon of 16 April his wife came home after being away since early morning. Walker asked her where she had been and she said she had gone to visit Sarah. He asked her how she had managed to find the home. Ann said she had taken from his pocket a note with the address on it. He told her she had no right to do anything of the sort and then accused her of pawning some of his clothes. Walker said he then put on his hat and told her he would leave the house and have nothing more to do with her, as he had given her a last chance. As he was going out of the door Mrs Walker said: 'Don't go. Give me one more chance and I'll be better for the future'. She tried to pull him back from the door but he broke loose, walked out, and banged the door after himself.

James Walker said that as he walked along the lobby he heard his wife cry out 'Oh!' Going back into the room, he found that she had cut her throat. He lifted her so he could look at the wound. She was bleeding profusely from a neck wound. He thought she was dead and, he said, he went to Mrs Godfrey's room and told her what his wife had done. He denied inflicting the wound. Asked by Mr Ford if he saw his wife use the razor or see her fall, Walker said he did not. He also did not run for a doctor because, he said, he was 'taken all aback'.

Speaking to the jury, Mr Le Mesurier stressed the evidence that Ann Walker had threatened suicide. He also said she was angry to have been walked out on by her husband. He said: 'Hell hath no fury like a woman scorned'. In a fit of frenzy, said Mr Le Mesurier, she cut her own throat. What would the jury think? Was it murder or suicide? They took only ten minutes to decide that Ann Walker had killed herself. James Walker was found not guilty of murder and was acquitted.

A Shooting at Sutton, St Helens

On 6 August 1902 Michael Noonan died at his house in Sutton, St Helens, shot by James Shaw, 43. Was it murder, manslaughter or an accident? This was what the legal process had to decide.

Michael Noonan was a collier, aged about 29. On the evening of 6 August Noonan, his brother Thomas and Alfred Ashton met James Shaw in the Boilermakers Arms at Sutton. While they were in the public house they may have had some kind of disagreement. At about 10.15 p.m. Shaw and his friends left the pub and walked along Watery Lane, in the direction of Berry's Lane. A few minutes later, Noonan followed along the same route. When Noonan got as far as the corner of Watery Lane he found Shaw and his friends talking, and joined the group. Some quarrelsome words ensued. Michael Noonan went back to the pub and told his brother and Ashton what had happened. It was a dark night and Thomas and Ashton lost sight of Michael, but in a few minutes they heard a scuffle going on. They found Michael and one of Shaw's friends struggling on the roadway. Shaw and another man looked on. Then Thomas Noonan went to his brother's assistance and, while he was doing so, Shaw had a gun and fired it. Thomas Noonan fell, fatally wounded.

It took an inquest jury only nine minutes to decide that Shaw was guilty of wilful murder. Shaw came before the magistrate at Dale Street on Thursday 21 August. Before he was committed for trial at the assizes, Shaw read out a statement in his own defence, giving his version of the events leading up to Michael Noonan's death. Shaw said: 'I have not much to say. I loaded up the gun and had been out with it the morning before, but never got a shot, and I intended going out again on the Tuesday night and waiting for daylight. I put the gun in my inside pockets, one piece in each pocket, and I dare say I was careful that nobody should see it, because this summer I have not taken out a licence to carry a gun. I had taken them out in previous years, but my last one ran out on the 31 July, just five days before. I knew Rigby would be on the look out. He knew I had not renewed my licence. When the Noonans and Ashton followed me and my mates, and Dixon, Gaiter and Tarpey were all on the ground together, I thought I would leave them at it, and went towards home. Somebody called out something about me and the next I saw was the Noonans and Ashton following me up. I was still 150 yards, more or less, away from home. I had been laid up with rheumatism, and I was in no fit fettle, so as I saw them coming I fired my gun into the air. One of them, either Michael or Thomas Noonan, called out: 'We will have thee, and thy gun too!' They rushed towards me and we began struggling. Thomas Noonan hit me twice on the forehead and kicked me on the right hand twice, trying to get the gun off me. Michael Noonan got hold of it too, and it was in this struggle it went off, and shot Michael. There would not have been above five minutes between the two shots. I never aimed the gun point blank at Michael and I never wanted to shoot either him or anyone else. I have never been a man for using violence. All there is against me is taking a drop of drink now and again, and doing a bit of poaching. I came back to give myself up as soon as I heard anything serious had happened. I went to Warrington and then to Knutsford, unknowing that Noonan was dead, and thinking there would be more bother next day if I stopped at home. I have relatives in Knutsford and I often go over there.'

Before the magistrates retired for a few minutes to consider their decision, defence solicitor Mr Riley pleaded that the shooting was an accident. The magistrates left it to be decided by the jury at Shaw's trial, which opened at St George's Hall on 3 December 1902.

The principal witness for the prosecution at the trial was Thomas Noonan, whose accounts of the shooting contained some important differences from Shaw's version. Noonan said that on the night of the shooting, his brother Michael left home at 2 Back Berry's Lane about 7.15 p.m. with James Critchley. Later, Thomas left with Alfred Ashton and went to the Boilermakers Arms. There he saw his brother, Critchley, James Pender and Alfred Johnson sitting together in the tap room, and Shaw with three men – Thomas Tarpey, Fred Gaiter and James Dixon. During the half hour when they were in the pub there was no quarrel, said Thomas. No conversation took place between the two groups. Shaw and his three friends left the pub and, about ten minutes later, Michael Noonan went out. He came back after about a quarter of an hour and then went out again alone.

A couple of minutes later, Thomas and Ashton left the pub. They walked the 300 yards to the end of Rolling Mill Lane. Michael was in sight in front of them. The nearest way home was to the right, along Watery Lane. Thomas was about 50 yards from the end of Rolling Mill Lane when he saw Michael turn to the right, up the lane. Thomas and Ashton followed. Michael went out of their sight and they heard a scuffle in the darkness. They found Michael and Dixon wrestling on the ground in front of Twist's house. Shaw, Tarpey and Gaiter were standing about three yards away. Thomas tried to lift his brother up, but failed. When he turned round from the men, Shaw had gone. Michael said something about Gaiter, and a general scuffle ensued.

Then Thomas Noonan, Michael Noonan and Ashton walked away from the other three men. They walked about 25 yards, close to the turn into Nook Lane, when they saw Shaw. Michael was in front. When Shaw came to about 20 yards away, Michael called out to Thomas: 'Here's Jim Shaw!' Thomas replied: 'Come on home; never mind Jim Shaw.' Shaw was approaching. When he was eight to ten yards away, Thomas saw Shaw pull one half of a gun out of one side of his jacket, and the other half out of the other inside pocket. He said he saw Shaw put the gun together. Shaw came up to about a yard from Michael. The muzzle of the double barrelled gun was only a few inches from Michael. Thomas said he saw Shaw fire. Michael fell. As he fired, Shaw said: 'Yes, here's Shaw!'

Thomas Noonan said he tried to lift his brother as soon as he had dropped. On looking round, he saw Shaw with the gun. He knocked Shaw down, but Shaw immediately got up and pointed the gun at Thomas, saying: 'I will blow your brains out.' Thomas thought the gun was loaded and knelt down. He again hit Shaw and knocked him down. The gun fell to the ground. Thomas said he shouted to Ashton: 'Alf, get hold of that gun!' Ashton and Shaw then had a struggle and Ashton ultimately gained possession of the weapon. Shaw went off towards his home, but before leaving he said: 'I will fetch another gun and blow all three of your brains out'. Thomas went for medical help for his brother.

James Pender of 8 Elizabeth Street said he went along Rolling Mill Lane and heard a shot. He was going across a field when he heard a second shot. He thought there was about three or four minutes between the two shots. Several other witnesses spoke of hearing the two shots within a similar time gap.

Medical evidence was given by Dr Unsworth. He said the cause of death was bleeding and shock due to a gunshot wound from which 27 pellets were removed. The shot had entered the abdomen and come out on Noonan's right side above the groin. The doctor said he thought the gun was about a foot away from the body when it was fired. He believed the gun was more probably discharged during a struggle.

Shaw was arrested after fleeing to Knutsford and being persuaded to return home by his wife's mother. He was confronted by Constables Marsh and Littler who were watching his house. At 10.40 p.m. they saw Shaw with his mother-in-law coming across Sutton Moss. Marsh said to Shaw: 'You will have to come with me'. Shaw said: 'All right, I know all about it'. On the way to the police office, Shaw was alleged to have said: 'I didn't shoot him. It was Noonan's brother. The Noonans are a bad lot'.

At the trial, Shaw stuck to his evidence that the gun went off during his struggle with Noonan. The trial occupied two days. The jury took an hour to decide that Shaw was not guilty of any offence. He was released.

Gladstone Street

Francis Burke and Catherine Daly lived together as man and wife. For a while they had lived with Catherine's brother Matthew in a house on Arkwright Street, but because of their continual disagreements Matthew told them to leave. They moved to a house in a court off Gladstone Street, at the city end of Vauxhall Road. On 26 August 1902 in the early hours, Burke attacked Daly with a hatchet and afterwards cut her throat with a knife, followed by an attempted suicide by cutting his own throat. Catherine Daly died at the Northern Hospital on 1 September.

Burke stood trial for murder at St George's Hall on Friday 5 December 1902 before Mr Justice Jelf and a jury. John Shingler, a licensed peddler, rented rooms in the house occupied by Burke in Gladstone Street. He described Frank Burke as 'an inoffensive, hard-working, sober man'. On Monday evening, 25 August, Burke came home from work and found that Daly was out. He was perfectly sober and said to Shingler: 'I suppose Kate has gone out for something for tea'. When Kate came home later she was very drunk and had a black eye. Later in the evening Shingler heard the couple quarrelling, and also heard the voice of Burke's sister, Lizzie Caton. While he was in bed, Shingler heard the sound of furniture being overturned, and then a cry of 'Help!' On going downstairs to the scene of the quarrel, Shingler heard a woman cry out: 'Oh Frank you have done it at last!' Shingler found Kate Daly lying on her back. Blood was flowing from her head and also from a wound in her throat. Shingler said to Burke: 'Good God, what have you done?' Burke said nothing. Shingler thought the woman was dead. He went to the Northern Dispensary for a doctor. On his return, Shingler found Burke and Daly clasped in each other's arms. He separated them and held the woman on his shoulder until the doctor arrived.

Mrs Shingler described how Daly and Caton were together, drunk. She heard a cry of 'Murder!' and also heard Burke say: 'There, that finishes it.' When Mrs Shingler returned to Burke's room a little later, she found him in the act of cutting his throat with a long white-handled knife which he used to eat with. Burke survived but Kate Daly did not. Police Constable 104A was called to the house. He found Burke in a corner on the floor being restrained by several men. The woman was also on the floor, wounded in the throat and head. The constable asked Catherine who had caused the injuries. She pointed to Burke and said: 'He done it'.

On 30 August, Kate Daly made a statement, in the presence of two magistrates and of Burke, from her bed in the Northern Hospital. She said she was a single woman and had lived with Burke for the past seven years. On 25 August, she said, Burke came home and was in a rage with her because she had not got his tea ready. Neither of them, she said, were sober. High words ensued. Burke got a hatchet and hit her on the head with it three or four times. She said he also used a knife on her: 'He drew it across my neck and brought me to my senses. I screamed and a policeman and a detective came.' She said Burke had often assaulted her. On one occasion he had trampled upon her.

Burke recovered from his wounds in the Brownlow Hill Workhouse. He was committed for jury trial on 2 October. At his trial, Burke went into the witness box to give his version of the affair at Gladstone Street. He said that when he returned home from work on the evening of the 25th he found his wife was out. He went to see if she was at his sister Lizzie's house in nearby Naylor Street. He found his sister with a woman friend, the worse for drink. Lizzie went out and pawned a skirt and he shouted at her for pawning her clothes for drink. This did not prevent him, however, from having a cupful of rum himself at Lizzie's house. He then went back home to see if Kate had returned. She had not.

Burke said he cut some chips and fried them for his tea. While he was eating, Kate came home. He asked her to have some chips but she refused, saying she was drunk. He noticed she had a black eye, and when he asked her who gave it to her she said Mary Ann, meaning Mary Ann Daly, Kate's sister-in-law. Burke said that Kate would not eat any tea; he asked a neighbour to get some beer. Mrs Shingler came into the room and put a poultice on Kate's black eye. Burke said he sat on the doorstep and all the time Kate was thumping him over the head, of which he 'took no notice'. When Lizzie saw Kate thrashing him, she said: 'Frank, you must be cur to allow it.' Lizzie and Kate drank more and Lizzie began to call Frank names. Exasperated, Burke jumped up from the doorstep, caught hold of Kate and put her into a chair. He asked her to 'leave off'. Again, said Burke, he went to the step and Lizzie followed him. Kate renewed her attacks and pulled Burke down. He said to the court in evidence: 'From this time until I found myself the next day in the hospital, I remembered nothing more.' He also said: 'So far as I know I might have struck her a thousand times.'

Gladstone Street.
Liverpool Record Office, Liverpool Libraries and Information Services

When the jury returned to court after being out for twenty minutes, the foreman gave a verdict of 'guilty of manslaughter, under grave provocation'. Mr Justice Jelf sentenced Frank Burke to seven years penal servitude.

The Kensit Case

This case concerned John Kensit, a well known lecturer who toured the country presiding over and speaking at rallies and meetings to champion the cause of Protestantism. At Birkenhead on 25 September 1902, Kensit was struck on the head while making his way to the Woodside Ferry from a meeting in Claughton. He died in the Liverpool Royal Infirmary from meningitis and septic pneumonia set up by blood poisoning. On leaving the hall in Claughton, Kensit was put into a special tramcar with his friends with the intention of crossing to Liverpool by rail from Hamilton Square Station. Because of the large crowd at the station entrance, it was decided that the party should travel by ferryboat. When Kensit got out of the tram at the Woodside terminal, a piece of iron was thrown at him. He put his hand to his head and fell to the ground. The onlookers remembered the iron making a dreadful clanging sound as it hit the cobblestones.

The police arrested a black man, a labourer called John McKeever, aged 18. He was said to have had a piece of iron in his hand as he stood by a lamp post near the ferry. He was playing a mouth organ and keeping time to the tune by knocking the iron against the post. McKeever claimed he was holding a stick, not a piece of iron, but witnesses described the distinct metallic sound of his tapping. One witness said that McKeever was with a group of girls. As Kensit's party approached the landing stage, one of the girls was alleged to have called out: 'Nigger, when he come along, let him have that'. Another witness said he saw McKeever throw the iron.

John McKeever was tried at the assizes on Monday 8 December and the trial occupied the next three days as well. At 2.10 p.m. on the final day, defence counsel Mr Madden rose to make his final speech to the jury. He pleaded that a man called McLaughlin had done the deed and confessed to it. McKeever, he said, was the innocent victim of mistaken identity. The jury were in consultation from 9.15 p.m. to 9.45 p.m. that night. They found McKeever not guilty. He was discharged, to scenes of unrestrained jubilation in the court and on the St George's plateau outside. Nobody else was charged with Kensit's murder.

The Smothered Spinster

On Wednesday 8 October 1902, an elderly unmarried lady called Elizabeth Marsden was found dead in her bed at 27 Oriel Road in Bootle. Because of the complex nature of the case, the inquest into Miss Marsden's death had to be adjourned several times. Eventually, the inquest proceeded to a conclusion on Tuesday 25 November at the Bootle Police Buildings in Oriel Road. By then the police had completed their interviews of potential witnesses. As a result of police inquiries, three young women had been arrested and charged with being concerned in Miss Marsden's death. Eliza

Hamilton, aged 19, had first been charged with stealing clothing from Miss Marsden. From a statement made by Hamilton, two others were implicated. They were Eva Eastwood, 17, and Ethel Rollinson, aged 20. All three were present at the inquest but by their light-hearted manner in court, they seemed to be either unaware or oblivious to the seriousness of their situation.

Mary Kershaw of 56 Clifford Street said that she had occasionally worked for Miss Marsden at her house in Oriel Road during the previous year or so. She saw Miss Marsden on the morning of 7 October. On the old lady's instructions, Mary went with Eliza Hamilton to the house with the intention of Eliza being taken on as a domestic servant. Eliza was told to start work the following day, Wednesday 8 October. The next morning, Eliza left home at Clifford Street and Mary Kershaw went with her as far as Oriel Road. Eliza said she would try to get on with Miss Marsden even though she didn't like the old lady very much.

At about midnight on the 8th, Eliza called on Mary, looking very down-hearted as if she had been crying. She told Mary that she let two girls into Miss Marsden's house. They put pillows over her face and stole two purses. They had given Eliza some of the stolen money and a parcel of clothes. The two girls said they had come to 'do it' to the old lady. Mary asked Eliza if she had reported the matter at the town hall police office. Eliza replied: 'No, I am frightened.' Mary went back with Eliza to Oriel Road. They saw a parcel lying in the garden. Mary said they did not touch the parcel, but went to the bridewell and told the police. Later on, Mary found a two shilling piece on the mantelpiece in Eliza's bedroom. It was Eliza's first job in service and Mary said she was usually cheerful with a pleasant disposition.

Police Constable Odlin said that at about 12.50 a.m. on the morning of 9 August he was leaving the Central Police Office when he met Mary Kershaw. He said she was carrying a parcel of clothing wrapped in brown paper. From what she told him, Odlin went to 27 Oriel Road with Constable Slattery. They knocked but got no answer. The house was in darkness. He and Slattery got in through the back. The ground floor rooms were in order but the front bedroom was a shambles. The contents of the wardrobe and drawers were strewn around the room. Miss Marsden was lying in bed on her back. The bedclothes were up to her chin, her head hidden from view. Lying across her face was a pillow, then a bolster on top of that, then another pillow and a cardboard box on top of all. The body was warm.

Odlin applied artificial respiration but to no avail. Slattery went for Dr Pearson who found that Miss Marsden had died. At about 2.00 p.m. Police Constable Odlin and Sergeant Flanagan went to 56 Clifford Street and took Eliza Hamilton to the police office.

Detective Constable Dixon wrote down a statement from Eliza on 10 October. Eliza said that Miss Marsden was getting on to her in the bedroom and shouted at her. Eliza said: 'I bought her a bottle of gin from a shop in Stanley Road.' She had stout and oysters for supper. Miss Marsden said to Eliza: 'You are standing like a post and are no good. What do I pay you for?' Then Eliza undressed the old lady and put her to bed. Eliza said that when she thought Miss Marsden was asleep she put the pillow on her face 'in a fit of passion'. She took some clothes and left the house. Being frightened to carry the parcel she left it on the steps.

Dixon spoke to Eva Eastwood and Ethel Rollinson on 15 November while they were waiting for a train on the overhead railway. Rollinson allegedly said: 'The old bat starved me when I was with her. I said I would do it, and I have done it. Eliza Hamilton helped. She can't say she didn't'. Turning to Eastwood, Rollinson said: 'We didn't get much out of it, did we? We read about it in the paper and thought about giving ourselves up on Monday.' On searching through a house in Beaufort Street, Dixon found some of Miss Marsden's clothes and a pawn ticket for some of her property. When the three women were charged with causing Miss Marsden's death, Eliza Hamilton kept silent. Ethel Rollinson, turning to Eliza, said: 'This woman is not in it.' Eva Eastwood, pointing to Rollinson, said: 'It is only between us two.'

There was further incriminating evidence against Rollinson and Eastwood. Mrs Mary Lees of Argos Road said Rollinson told her that when she left Miss Marsden she was going to give her 'a lamb-basting'. To Esther Wilkinson of Brasenose Road, Rollinson said: 'I know an old lady with plenty of money, a wardrobe full of gold. What do you say if we knock the old lady down and break in?' Rollinson had said she intended to drug and rob Miss Marsden. On 23 October, Sarah Hall met Rollinson and Eastwood in Moss Street. Eastwood said: 'I am in it. I helped to do it'. The clothes had been pledged with pawnbrokers in Great Crosshall Street and Great Homer Street.

The inquest jury gave a verdict of wilful murder against the three accused women – Rollinson, Eastwood and Hamilton. At the committal hearing on 26 November, all three were ordered to stand trial at the assizes. However, Eliza Hamilton turned King's evidence. She was freed from prosecution by agreeing to testify against the other two women. It was chiefly because of Hamilton's evidence that Rollinson and Eastwood were, on 13 December, convicted of murder and sentenced to death. The jury added a recommendation to mercy 'on account of their youth and sex'. The execution date was fixed for 31 December, but before then Rollinson and Eastwood were both reprieved and had their death sentences commuted to life imprisonment.

Murder carried a mandatory death sentence until 1957. Many juries were reluctant to find a person guilty if there were any doubts about the case, or if the case was one of tragedy rather than maliciousness or evil. Juries would in some cases give a verdict of guilty of murder but recommend mercy. Whether mercy would be shown was at the discretion of the judge and the Home Secretary.

⚘ 1903 ⚘

Peach Street

At about 6.30 a.m. on the morning of Monday 16 February 1903, Police Constable John Jones was on duty on Brownlow Hill when he was approached by a man called William Smith, a 52-year-old labourer who lived nearby at 26 Peach Street. Smith told Jones that his wife Isabella had fallen down dead. When Jones got to the house he found Mrs Smith, 42, lying on a sofa in the front cellar kitchen. There was a wound on the left side of her chest. Smith said to Jones: 'She fell into the ash pan. I did not use a knife, officer.' Knife or not, Mrs Smith had lost a great deal of blood and there was bloodstained clothing in the kitchen and parlour. Smith, obviously shaken, said: 'Do you think there is anything wrong? There is nothing wrong here.' Smith's words belied the tragedy that was about to unfold at Peach Street.

The house was home to three families. The Smiths and their children occupied the front parlour and two cellars. The other rooms were occupied by Mrs Smith's eldest daughter, Mary Jane Wyness, her husband and their children, and two rooms were home to a woman called Eliza Byrne and her husband George. It was Mary Jane who identified her mother's body at the Princes Dock Mortuary, and it was she who was the first witness at an inquest at Dale Street Police Buildings on Friday 27 February.

Mary Jane said her mother was a fairly healthy woman, but she was badly addicted to drink. Her father William Smith also drank heavily and often beat her mother during the course of regular disagreements. Her mother had been drinking more heavily than usual in recent weeks. On the afternoon of 15 February, Mary Jane saw her mother and father slightly drunk but on good terms. Afterwards she heard her mother nagging her father because he would not give her any of the money he had won betting but had spent it on other people. At 3.30 a.m. the next morning, Mary Jane heard moans coming from the cellar. She went downstairs to the cellar kitchen, where she found her mother lying face downwards on the floor, with her head on the ash pan of the fireplace. Mrs Smith wore a chemise, blouse and stockings. Mary Jane ran upstairs to the front parlour and called her father, who was asleep in bed. Father and daughter went down to the cellar and lifted Mrs Smith onto the sofa. She was bleeding from the left side of her chest. Her clothes were covered in blood and she was unconscious. Mary Jane asked George Byrne to go for a doctor but he returned without one, so he and Mr Smith went for a policeman. On the way back, Byrne asked Smith how Mrs Smith had got injured. Smith replied: 'I don't know any more than you do.'

Mary Jane's husband, Henry Wyness, was lying in bed recovering from a fever, so he didn't go down to the cellar at first, but he did hear someone falling and moaning noises. Soon after Mary Jane had gone down, Henry heard her cry out: 'Oh, my Mammy!' Smith came up to the top landing and shouted: 'Come downstairs, my wife is dying!' Later he was told Mrs Smith was dead.

Smith also went to the bedroom occupied by the Byrnes. According to Mr Byrne, Smith came up and shouted: 'George, get up, my wife is dead!' However, Mrs Byrne's 11-year-old daughter told a police sergeant that Smith said: 'George, George, I have killed my wife!' Only two days before, Mrs Smith had been helping to celebrate the Wynesses' wedding anniversary. Eliza Byrne said that she and Isabella Smith drank nine quarts of beer between them from 2.00 p.m. to 10.30 p.m. on Saturday the 14th.

William Smith was taken into custody and put into a cell at Prescot Street where he was locked up with four other men. One of these men, William Needham, asked Smith what he was in for. 'Murder', said Smith. 'I struck my wife with a poker, but I did not mean to kill her. You know a woman's breast is very tender, and it went in.' Asked why he had done it, Smith said: 'I was driven to it. She hasn't been sober since Christmas.' A poker was found near the fireplace in the cellar. It had recently been washed and cleaned. Forensic evidence showed that Mrs Smith died almost immediately from a wound between the first and second ribs, one inch diameter and 4½ inches deep. Dr Nathan Raw, who did the post mortem examination, said a deep wound had penetrated the pulmonary artery, causing massive bleeding. Dr Raw said it was possibly caused by the poker and that the wound would have required 'violent muscular force, in fact, extraordinary force'. It could not have been caused by a fall on to the ash pan.

A two-day committal hearing in March led to William Smith's trial on 8 May before Mr Justice Lawrance. In their 26-year marriage, Smith had three times been convicted of assaulting his wife – in 1886, 1899 and in 1900. The jury returned a verdict of manslaughter. The judge said he agreed with the verdict because of the provocation suffered by Smith owning to his wife's heavy drinking. Smith was sentenced to twelve years penal servitude.

Altcar Camp

Early on Sunday morning, 17 May, Royal Welch Fusilier Private Frederick Boswell was returning to Altcar Camp after a night out in nearby Formby. It was about 3.30 a.m. and, because in 1903 British Summer Time had not yet been devised, day had already broken as Boswell made his way along a rough path, known locally as the 'Black Path' or 'Fisherman's Walk'. He was about half a mile from the camp when he heard the sound of someone groaning coming from a ditch which ran beside the path. A soldier lay face downwards in the ditch, in two or three inches of water. His head and face were badly injured. Boswell turned the man over and put him on a dry area before going to camp for help. Sergeant Jenkins, instructor of musketry, prepared a stretcher and the injured man was conveyed to the camp hospital. He groaned now and again on the way. When the man was being put into a bed, he breathed his last with a huge sigh and died.

Dr Francis Carter of Formby examined the body. The dead soldier was Private John James, also of the Royal Welch Fusiliers. He had sustained some sixteen gaping wounds to his face, head, hands and fingers, probably caused by the buckle of a belt found about twenty yards from the body, in Dickenson's Field. The dead man's watch was missing. His nasal bones were crushed and the lobe of his right ear was almost severed. His skull was fractured.

Later that morning the corps of 66 men fell in for Sergeant Jenkins, who inspected each man's belt for certain identity marks. The belt belonging to Private William Burke was missing. It was being worn by Private Arthur Wilkes and had been tampered with. The buckle had been flattened, one prong had been broken and the number '20' scratched off. Wilkes was improperly dressed for Sunday parade, as instead of wearing his regimental trousers he had turned up in his blue fatigue trousers. He stood out like a sore thumb. Sgt. Jenkins bellowed at Wilkes: 'What are you doing on parade in them trousers? Why are you not wearing your regimentals?' Wilkes said they were in his kit bag in his tent. Jenkins went and found a pair of trousers and he said to Wilkes: 'Are those them?' Wilkes replied: 'Yes sir, them is mine.' The trousers had been sold to Wilkes by Private Bullen at about 8.00 a.m. that very morning. Sgt. Jenkins threw them to Wilkes, who put them on, and Wilkes was arrested and locked up at Formby police station.

Arthur Wilkes was under suspicion, however, even before the Sunday assembly. On Saturday afternoon, Private Burke hung his belt on a peg in his tent, ready for the following morning's parade. On Sunday morning it was missing, a fact which he reported to his lance corporal. Lance Corporal Stevenson, just before 6.00 a.m. on the Sunday morning, was awakened by someone coming into his tent. He then saw a man going out of the tent very quickly. It was Wilkes. Later, Stevenson and Burke went to Wilkes's tent where there was a belt hanging up. Burke said: 'That is my belt.' Wilkes said: 'No it is not.' Stevenson said: 'Didn't you go out with James last night?' Wilkes replied: 'Shut up. If they hear you they will think I had something to do with it. I don't want anything to do with a case like that.' Wilkes was upset, flushed and agitated. His missing regimental trousers were found hidden behind some equipment in the store tent on Monday morning. They were dirty, torn and damp.

On Tuesday 19 May an inquest was opened at the Railway Hotel in Formby. County Coroner Brighouse ordered James's body to be put back where it was found so that an inquest jury could fulfil their duty of viewing the remains and could examine the surroundings. Dr Carter was told to accompany them to answer any questions. When looking at the body, one juryman fainted at the gruesome sight before the jury made their way back to the comfort of the Railway Hotel.

A week later the inquest was resumed at the police buildings in Birkdale. Just before the start of the hearing of evidence, Wilkes made a statement, taken down and read out by Inspector Hodgson. The statement read:

> On the night we went out me and James went in several beershops until we both got drunk. The last beerhouse we went in was the Railway Hotel. I called for a quart of beer. When we drank that, James called for a quart and they told us we had had enough. I said to James: 'Come away, we will get back to camp

now'. We were talking friendly all the way until we got near to the camp ground but all of a minute James stopped and said to me: 'We will go back again and get some more beer.' I said: 'No, we have had enough. We will go to the camp and get to bed. If we go back they won't serve us and we might get locked up for being drunk.' I got hold of his arm in a friendly manner and tried to get him to camp. We started wrestling and he got vexed and said: 'You will have to go to the front and get some medals on your chest before you can stop me going back into town.' While we were wrestling he tore my trousers and got me vexed and him being a stronger man than me, I was anxious to get out of his clutch for fear he might do me harm. I could not get out of his clutch so I had to use my belt to make him lose his grip and he did so then. I left him and went back to camp, not knowing what I had done to him.

After the close of the inquest, next day, Wilkes appeared before the magistrates at Birkdale. Additional evidence was given by Private George Bellhouse, who said that on the Sunday at 7.00 a.m., he went to Wilkes's tent. Wilkes was lying on two forms with a blanket over him. Bellhouse woke Wilkes and said to him: 'Bogie, have you heard?'

'No, what?' asked Wilkes.

'One of the cooks is missing and they have found him murdered in yonder field.'

'Get out,' said Wilkes. 'It's a good job I did not come home with him, or I might have been blamed.'

Arthur Wilkes was tried at the Liverpool Summer Assizes on 31 July 1903. He pleaded 'not guilty in self defence'. Not a single mark of violence was found on Wilkes. Also it was generally agreed that Wilkes was much stronger and more powerful than the unfortunate John James. For the defence, Mr Sharpe claimed that Wilkes acted in self-defence after being attacked and under the influence of drink. In his summing up, which lasted from 2.30 to 3.30 p.m., Mr Justice Bigham said there was no evidence that Wilkes was defending himself. He described the killing as 'a wicked and brutal murder'. At 4.15 p.m. the jury returned with a 'guilty' verdict, with a recommendation to mercy, on account of Wilkes's youth (he was 21). After pronouncing the death sentence, the judge advised Wilkes not to rely on mercy because, he said: 'Personally I can hold out no hope of mercy.'

Private John James was born in a village near Swansea. He enlisted in 1898 at the age of 24 and saw active service in South Africa, receiving a medal with five clasps. In 1900 he was transferred to China, from where he was invalided home in January 1902. Stationed at Lichfield, he had been sent to Altcar for musketry training. Wilkes was a recruit who had seen no active service.

On Monday 10 August, copies of a reprieve petition for Wilkes were placed for signature at St George's Hall, Simpson's on the Landing Stage, and at the office of defence solicitor Edward Lloyd at 41 North John Street. The total number of signatures, collected on the 10th and sent to the Home Secretary that evening, was 1,665. Mr Lloyd described it as 'an influential petition'.

The execution was fixed to take place on Tuesday morning, 18 August. By Friday the 14th no reprieve had arrived. Wilkes was visited for the second time by his mother, who had travelled up from Birmingham. He was reported to be 'very quiet' and as giving 'no trouble whatsoever'. He had been receiving advice and counselling by Anglican Chaplain Rev. Morris. On Saturday 15 August a letter from the Home Secretary was received by solicitor Lloyd. It read: 'Sir – In reply to the petitions transmitted by you on behalf of Arthur Wilkes, who is now lying under sentence of death in His Majesty's Prison at Liverpool, I am instructed by the Home Secretary to acquaint you that he feels warranted in all the circumstances in advising His Majesty to respite the capital sentence with a view of commutation to penal servitude for life – I am sir, your obedient servant, C. E. Troup'. Wilkes's life had been spared.

The Blundellsands Children

Joseph Cannell, a plasterer, had been married to his wife Eleanor for fourteen years. They had five children. In May 1903 Mr Cannell and his two sons Willie and Alfred slept in one bedroom of their house at 3 Brighton Vale in Blundellsands. Mrs Cannell and their daughter Jane used another room. On Sunday morning, 31 May, Mr Cannell left the house at 8.50 a.m. to go for a walk. He hadn't seen Eleanor that morning. He got back home at 2.00 p.m. Going in through the back door, he met his wife, who said: 'The children are in a tub and I have taken poison'. Mrs Cannell was in a frantic state. Joseph looked into the cradle and the bassinet, but the two youngest children – Alfred Edward, aged 18 months, and Eleanor Leonora

(6 months) were not there. He went into the back kitchen. The two children were lying face downwards in a dolly tub where Mrs Cannell did her washing. They had drowned in eighteen inches of water.

Mrs Cannell was in the front bedroom. A rope was tied around her neck. On end she had fastened to a bedpost. She was trying to strangle herself. Mr Cannell released her and she ran into another room with a table knife in her hand. She tried to cut her throat with it. He had to hold her to stop her injuring herself. Then she pleaded with him to let her go to the shore to drown herself.

Eleanor Cannell had been behaving oddly in recent weeks. She thought her husband had taken a dislike to her and the youngest child. Mr Cannell had occasionally stayed off work to see that she didn't do herself any harm. She was constantly studying reports of suicides in the newspapers. She had often threatened to do something to the children. Many a time Eleanor had told Joseph, when he went out in the morning, that he would not see the babies when he came back. Now it had happened. Only the day before, she came into a pub where Joseph was having a drink, picked up his glass and threw the beer into his face.

Dr Reid arrived at the house at 2.40 p.m. He found Eleanor upstairs lying on a bed. One end of the bedpost was slightly dislodged, the rope still fastened to it. She was in a terrible mental condition and was vomiting at intervals. The doctor had her taken to hospital under sedation. In Eleanor's clothes was the following letter: 'My dearest father – When you hear what has happened I know you will be sorry for my unhappiness, if nobody else will. I cannot live in such trouble. Forgive me and don't blame me too much – your unhappy daughter, Eleanor.'

Mrs Cannell had to undergo full legal process for the killing of her two children. An inquest jury found her guilty of wilful murder and at a hearing at the County Sessions House on William Brown Street on 16 June she was ordered to stand trial for murder. In the dock she cried bitterly, calling at intervals for her children.

In 1823 Judges were allowed merely to record sentences of death in court and so commute them on the spot. In tragic cases where the prisoner had not deliberately or maliciously committed murder, such as in the case of infanticide, they were not then subjected to the terrifying ordeal of being told they were to be hanged. However, in 1861, this procedure was ended and Judges had to pronounce the death sentence from the bench. Several attempts were made to change this, the last being in 1909, but without success. Directing the jury to return a verdict of 'guilty but insane' or of manslaughter was not only just, but prevented additional distress to the prisoner.

At the Liverpool Summer Assizes in 1903, Eleanor Cannell's trial was brief. Dr Price of Walton Prison testified that in his opinion she was suffering from melancholia and could not on her own initiative direct a proper defence for herself. Mr Justice Bigham then directed the jury to say she was unfit to plead to a charge of murder. This they did and Mrs Cannell was removed from public view.

Salisbury Street

At 10.00 p.m. on Tuesday evening, 2 June 1903, 12-year-old Mary Jane Lyon, after having been out to play, came home to 121 Salisbury Street, off Islington. When she got home, her mother asked her to take Mrs Margaret Constantine home to 28A Birchfield Street because the woman was the worse for drink. When Mary Jane was coming home again a little girl told her that her father had been stabbed. He was lying on the sofa. Mrs Lyon was sitting in a chair, crying. He was taken by ambulance to the Royal Infirmary but died later from a stab wound.

When Mary Jane was out with Mrs Constantine, her brother, 8-year-old Charles Lyon, was left with his father and mother, both of whom had been drinking. Little Charlie was on the sofa while his mother was sitting at the table, cutting bread. His father said to his mother: 'Kate, you've not mended my trousers right.' His mother made a muttering sound, as if she was saying something to herself. Mr Lyon then stood up and hit his wife in the face with his hand and said: 'Cut the bread for the children.' Mrs Lyon started to mutter again, so he hit her again. Twice more. Mrs Lyon was standing by the table. The bread knife was in her hand when he husband hit her. She went to shove him back, and as she was pushing him the knife penetrated Mr Lyon's clothing and chest. He put his hand to his heart and fell into a sitting position on the sofa. Mrs Lyon ran to the front door and shouted: 'I have killed Charlie, I have killed him!' Passing the house at that moment was Henry Dowling. Catherine Lyon said to him: 'Come in and see what I have done to my husband.' Dowling went in and Mrs Lyon said: 'I did it, but God knows I did not intend to hurt him'. Mr Lyon was lying on the sofa with a wound in the left side of his chest. Catherine broke down in tears. Standing in the centre of the room, little Charlie said to Dowling: 'My Mamma done it.' Mary Jane came in from her errand to view the tragic scene.

Dr Nuttall of the Royal Infirmary found that Mr Lyon died from a five-inch deep wound which had penetrated his heart. Mrs Lyon told the arresting officer: 'We were quarrelling and I hit him with something but I don't know what.' When she was on the way to the detective office she told Sergeant Whitely: 'I did it, but I didn't mean to do him any harm.' When charged with murder Mrs Lyon said: 'I never did it.'

Following an inquest where the jury gave a 'wilful murder' verdict, Catherine Lyon was committed to stand trial for murder at the assizes. However, on

Salisbury Street.
Liverpool Record Office, Liverpool Libraries and Information Services

hearing the facts of the case, the grand jury rejected the murder charge and found a true bill against Mrs Lyon for the manslaughter of her husband. She was tried at the assizes on 4 August 1903, found guilty of manslaughter, and sentenced by Mr Justice Bigham to penal servitude for three years.

An Adopted Child

In March 1903 a Mrs Fitzgerald of Thornton Street in Litherland got a letter from a Nurse Rankin asking her to foster a baby and to go and see her. The nurse told Mrs Fitzgerald to go to a house in Stoneycroft, where arrangements would be made for her to collect the child. From Stoneycroft, Mrs Fitzgerald got a cab and drove to the corner of Moscow Drive. A nurse-maid was waiting there with a baby, which she handed over with a parcel of clothing. Mrs Fitzgerald took the child, a new-born girl, home with her. The father of the child had already been to see Mrs Fitzgerald and had agreed to pay her five shillings a week to look after the little girl. Not long afterwards, the infant was advertised for adoption in the *Liverpool Echo*. The person who answered the advert was a woman who lived in Dudley Road, Mossley Hill. Her name was Mrs Elizabeth Sturgeon.

Mrs Sturgeon called on Mrs Fitzgerald and said she was wanting to adopt a child but that this one was too young; she wanted one about twelve months old. Later, Mrs Sturgeon said she would take the child but Mrs Fitzgerald should look after her until she was seven months old, for six shillings a week. Eventually, on 6 June 1903, Mrs Sturgeon took the baby herself and employed Mrs Fitzgerald's daughter Eva to look after it at Dudley Road. She called the child Mabel Sturgeon. However, at the end of June, Mrs Sturgeon told Mrs Fitzgerald that the little girl's mother wanted Mabel back. Then, on 3 July, Mrs Sturgeon sacked Eva Fitzgerald for 'being a naughty girl and turning on the gas', something she denied. On 7 July Mrs Sturgeon took the child with her to visit her own mother in Spalding, Lincolnshire. On arriving there, she wrote a letter to Mr Sturgeon. It was just the sort of letter an affectionate mother would write about her adopted child.

While at Spalding, Mrs Sturgeon engaged a young girl who was to play a major role in the case. Her name was Alice Porter. The idea was that Alice should look after the child back in Dudley Road now that Eva Fitzgerald had been dispensed with. Mrs Sturgeon wrote a second affectionate letter to her husband Bill, telling him the train on which she would return and saying that the child had been christened. Mrs Sturgeon, Alice Porter and little Mabel arrived back at Dudley Road on 11 July. Less than three weeks later, on the morning of 30 July, the body of Mabel, aged 4½ months, was found in a lime heap in Solomon's Lane, Allerton.

The story of Mabel Sturgeon's death was revealed at an inquest held on 7 August. Of particular interest was the evidence of young Alice Porter who was close to the child in its final hours. Charged with murder and in custody was Mrs Sturgeon, accused of doing away with her adopted daughter.

On 28 July, Mrs Sturgeon sent Alice Porter to buy her a bottle of gin. After dinner, Mrs Sturgeon went to her bedroom for a lie down. When Bill Sturgeon heard of this he asked Alice if she had given his wife any drink. She said she had not done so. He went upstairs for a few minutes, then left the house. After Mr Sturgeon had gone out, Mrs Sturgeon told Alice that he had been in a vile temper, although Alice herself had seen no sign of this. Later in the day, Elizabeth Sturgeon wrote two letters, one of which – to her father and mother – was very peculiar. In the letter she wrote: 'Alice, baby and myself are going for our last walk after the cruelty of my husband.' She also wrote that Bill had tried to strangle her 'for the sake of a flower girl on the streets of Liverpool'.

At 4.00 p.m. on 28 July, Mrs Sturgeon decided that she would take little Mabel and Alice Porter for a walk. As it turned out, the walk would be a very long one. They set off and went to a field by Mossley Hill Church, and then went and sat under a hedgerow in another field. The baby began to cry and Mrs Sturgeon took it into her arms. The child cried, and then cried in what Alice Porter thought was 'a funny way'. Alice was sitting just behind her mistress. As she leaned forward, Alice saw Mrs Sturgeon put a handkerchief into the baby's mouth. She said it was to stop Mabel crying, but Alice protested and said: 'You will suffocate her.' After a few minutes the baby was silent. Mrs Sturgeon said it had gone to sleep. She wrapped the baby in Alice's jacket. As it went dark, Alice fell asleep and did not wake up until daybreak.

Next morning, they returned to Mossley Hill along the main road. When they came to the gate of a field, Mrs Sturgeon took a bottle from behind the gatepost. She said it had rum in it. She drank some and gave

Alice some. A man passed and said 'Good morning'. With Mrs Sturgeon carrying the baby in Alice's jacket, they went along a lane leading to a footbridge spanning the railway cutting at Mossley Hill. They sat by the bridge with the baby, still silent, lying on the ground. Then Mrs Sturgeon asked Alice to walk along the side parapet of the bridge and said she would give her a shilling. It was as if she was trying to put the girl into danger and sure enough Alice fell from the bridge on to the railway line. She sprained her ankle very badly. Mrs Sturgeon helped her over the lines and Alice crawled back up the embankment down which she had just fallen.

Mrs Sturgeon had another idea. She would take the baby home and return to help Alice get home. Mrs Sturgeon didn't go home. She was spotted by a man called Moore who was looking out of his window on the corner of a road leading to Solomon's Lane. It was in a nearby lime heap that the dead child was discovered the next day.

Mrs Sturgeon and Alice went home without Mabel. Mrs Sturgeon said the child had been left in the charge of a woman 'aged about forty in a black shawl and a black hat'. They called at John Heslop's milkhouse at Greenhill Farm in Booker's Lane. He had noticed them the previous day just before nightfall. Mrs Surgeon had no money with her so she gave Heslop her address. Then she sent Alice home, saying that Alice was to give her love to Mr Sturgeon. 'Goodbye Alice, and be a good girl', she said.

Alone now, Mrs Sturgeon went to the cab stand at the Brook House Hotel in Smithdown Road and hired a cab driven by Fred Leighton. She asked him to drive her to Dudley Road and then to Heslop's Farm in Allerton. She said she was looking for a child taken by a lady in black.

The inquest verdict was 'wilful murder'. Elizabeth Sturgeon faced trial at the assizes on 4 December 1903. Prosecution and defence agreed to accept the medical evidence of insanity. Bill Sturgeon testified to his wife's unusual behaviour over a lengthy period. He said he had noticed 'curious looks' in his wife's eyes for some time. She had, earlier in the year, given birth to a stillborn child. Her disappointment, said Mr Sturgeon, had been intense. She had a history of sleepwalking and of rushing out of the house for no apparent reason. Once he found her lying on a bed with an open razor, as if she was contemplating injuring herself. In spite of this testimony, Bill Sturgeon said he believed his wife was sane. The jury thought otherwise. The verdict was 'guilty but insane'. Mr Justice Ridley ordered Elizabeth Sturgeon to be confined as a criminal lunatic until His Majesty's pleasure be known.

Lyons Street, Bootle

On 1 December 1903 the trial was held of James McGuirk, 23, a fireman, and Elizabeth Watson, 26, a factory worker. They were brother and sister and were charged with the murder of Margaret Donoghue, 25, a bag sorter, of Bostock Street in Bootle. She died at Bootle Hospital as a result of terrible head injuries sustained at a house in Lyons Street on the night of 26 September.

During the day of the 26th, Donoghue spent most of the time drinking. At 8.00 p.m. she was sitting on the doorstep of Mrs Foy's house at No. 92 Lyons Street, along with Mrs Foy, a woman called Mary Ann White and another woman. Donoghue asked the others to have a drink and her sister Jane (15) went for some beer. One of the women suggested Donoghue should let Elizabeth Watson have some drink, whereupon Mary Ann White said: 'Don't give the little spitfire any.' A quarrel then ensued between Donoghue and Watson about the stealing of somebody else's beer. It ended with the two women going to 60 Lyons Street.

When they arrived at No. 60, Mrs McGuirk, the mother of the accused, and Maria O'Keefe were in the house, but they left shortly afterwards, leaving Donoghue and Watson together. Soon afterwards, Mary Ann White was passing the cellar of No. 60 when she heard a voice crying 'Oh James!' Then James McGuirk came out of the cellar, and after sitting a few minutes on some railings, he went across the street to No. 29, where his sister Mary Size lived. He said to Mary: 'Do you know who is over at our house? I have been after giving her a dishing out.'

Mary Size went for the police, who went to No. 60, where they found the door of the cellar fastened. McGuirk then arrived and opened the door for the police. The policemen discovered Margaret Donoghue lying on a settee under the window. Her head was in a pool of blood, and there was blood on the floor, walls, curtains and blinds. The woman was removed to hospital, where she died at about midnight from a skull fracture. On her head were four lacerated wounds. Her left ear was pierced through.

It seemed clear that Donoghue had come to her death at the hands of one of the prisoners, or both of them. All wounds had been caused by the same blunt instrument, and it was thought that the heel of a boot worn by McGuirk was likely to have caused such wounds. The boots, examined by the police, were smeared with blood, as was the clothing worn by both McGuirk and Watson.

At the inquest held in October, Elizabeth Watson's statement, made to Police Constable Jordan on the night of the killing, was read out:

> On Saturday night, the 26th, I met Margaret Donoghue, the deceased, in Lyons Street at Mrs Foy's door. We came up the street together and went into our cellar. We were not many minutes in when my brother James came in. Margaret was sitting on the settle when James came in. James said: 'Are you here?' He sprang at her, seized her by the throat, and threw her down on the settle. James then got on to the settle and stamped on her face and head with one foot. The deceased moaned, and was in a pool of blood. He stamped on her for about two minutes. I said 'James, don't do that!' He then made at me and I ran out to Size's house.

After the lunch adjournment at the trial, prosecuting counsel Mr Maxwell withdrew the case against Watson because, he said, no jury could take the view, on the doctor's evidence, that she inflicted any injuries. In defence of McGuirk, Mr Lord said there was insufficient evidence against McGuirk to ensure conviction. His disappearance after the crime was due to his anxiety over an unpaid fine.

The judge, Mr Justice Ridley, summed up in McGuirk's favour. The jury, without retiring, found him guilty of manslaughter. At this, the prisoner said nonchalantly: 'Verdict of manslaughter! All right!' The judge severely rebuked McGuirk. He said: 'I think you treat this case in a somewhat light-hearted manner. By your abominable violence you rushed upon this woman and took away her life. I think you are a fortunate man in that we have been able to find – partly on the circumstances that no one who actually witnessed the crime has been called against you – the means of reducing the case to manslaughter, but it remains a very bad case of manslaughter, and I pass upon you the sentence of fourteen years penal servitude.' McGuirk cried out: 'Fourteen years!' Two warders got hold of him and led him down to the cells. As he disappeared he shouted out, probably to Maria O'Keefe: 'Keep your heart up, Maria!'

⁂ 1904 ⁂

Great Newton Street

Mary Pike, 25, the wife of an able seaman of Great Newton Street, died in the Royal Infirmary on 4 March 1904 from the effects of a revolver shot alleged to have been fired by her brother-in-law, sailor William Kirwan, 39. Kirwan came to trial for murder on Monday 9 May 1904 before Mr Justice Bucknill.

Kirwan lived with his wife in Richmond Row. About May 1903, Kirwan suspected that his wife was going to Mary Pike's house to consort with a man. He complained to his wife and to Mary of his suspicions but both women denied his accusations.

On 25 February 1904, Kirwan called at Mary Pike's house and asked for her. They had some conversation about Kirwan borrowing her rent book. Next afternoon, the 26th, there were gunshots. John Russell, a cotton porter, was in his room at No. 31 at the time. He heard three loud bangs in quick succession, followed by the screams of women and children. On going downstairs, Russell saw Mary Pike with her two children standing near the front parlour door, with Kirwan also standing in the lobby with a revolver in his hand. He was pointing it towards the stairs. Mary was at the foot of the stairs. She shouted that Kitty Kirwan was in the parlour, shot. Russell burst open the parlour door and saw Mrs Kirwan standing there. He got hold of the two women and pushed them along the passage, standing himself between Kirwan and the two women. He then pushed Kirwan out of the house and locked him out.

Mrs Russell, looking out of an upstairs window, saw Kirwan on the doorstep, loading his revolver. He walked off towards Pembroke Place. On the way Kirwan discharged his revolver, apparently at no one in particular. He met a man called Robert Teare, a stonemason's labourer who lived at No. 29, to whom he complained of his wife's conduct, saying the house No. 31 was nothing less than a disorderly house.

A policeman, number 243B, came upon the scene. Kirwan was pointed out to him as the man with the gun. Kirwan was standing on the footpath

Great Newton Street in the 1960s
Liverpool Record Office, Liverpool Libraries and Information Services

outside No. 31 with his two hands in his trouser pockets. At this moment, Mary Pike was inside, in the lobby. Russell said to her: 'It's all right now, the policeman has got him. You had better go and charge him'. Mary opened the door and went across the street towards Kirwan. When she had got near him, Kirwan pulled a hand out of his pocket and fired at Mrs Pike. She fell to the ground. As the policeman took the revolver from Kirwan, he said: 'Be careful, officer, it is still loaded.'

Kirwan was charged with attempting to murder both his wife and Mrs Pike. He said: 'I attempted to kill the pair of them. I am sorry I didn't; I meant it well enough.' When he was charged on 8 March with the murder of Mrs Pike, Kirwan said: 'I have nothing to say only I have been driven to it with great provocation' Mary Pike received a bullet wound on the left side of her body and a fractured rib on the right side. The bullet entered the left side and was found near the right rib. The cause of death, certified by Dr Robert Knowles of the Royal Infirmary, was pneumonia.

We now come to William Kirwan's version of events, as given in the evidence in his own defence. He said he went to Mary Pike's house, at his wife's urgent request for a rent book. Mary asked him if there was any trouble at his house and Kirwan replied: 'If there is, your sister is the cause of it.' On the following day his wife asked him to go with her to her sister's for the rent book. He followed her to Pike's house and some conversation ensued about the rent book. Kirwan said: 'If my wife had gone straight there would be no need of this.' Mrs Kirwan asked: 'What do you mean by going straight?' Kirwan then asked Mary if it was true about the letter from Sheffield, from a man his wife was friendly with. His wife said: 'Yes.' He then accused his wife of misconduct and she denied it. Kirwan then drew his revolver and fired three shots at his wife. He meant to shoot her and fired one shot at Mrs Pike. Kirwan then went into the lobby and said: 'You had better come out of that.' He went into the streets and, after putting two bullets in his revolver, he shouted to his wife: 'Come out, it's all right!' He said he meant that he wanted his wife to go home with him. The policeman came up and caught hold of him. The constable was very nervous. Someone shouted: 'Search him officer, he's got a revolver!' One said: 'That's the man, officer, he's got a revolver on him.' Then Mary Pike called him a foul name. Kirwan said: 'Why doesn't your sister come out and give me in charge?' She replied by calling him another foul name. He then drew the revolver and shot her.

In defence of Kirwan, Mr Madden said that he was not insane, but his mind had been disordered and had lost its balance. Mr Madden said: 'If there is one thing more than another which disorders a man's mind, it is jealousy. The prisoner, rightly or wrongly, believed that his wife was unfaithful, and he allowed his mind to be upset by that belief.'

The judge declared that the prisoner had admitted he shot Mary Pike and that the jury had no option but to return a verdict of murder. This they did without leaving the jury box. Asked if he had anything to say why sentence should not be passed on him, Kirwan said: 'In this dock I swear my wife is guilty. Before God I swear that she is guilty of all I have accused her of. Those witnesses against me can say so if they will. They have encouraged it.'

Passing sentence, the judge said he was sure that Kirwan thought his wife unfaithful, but that did not justify him in taking Mrs Pike's life. Kirwan, said the judge, had had the courage to admit in the witness box that he deliberately took her life, and for that act nothing remained but to pass sentence of death. The judge said to Kirwan: 'I can offer no hope at this side of the grave. I ask you to make peace with your Maker.'

As the death sentence was pronounced, Kirwan stood at the bar of the dock with his arms folded, perfectly composed. Before he went jauntily down the stairs he said: 'So long Sarah, goodbye to you and your husband. You have stood by me. Thank you and Mr Madden.' Just before the death sentence, an old woman, a relative of Kirwan, pathetically appealed for his release. So persistent were the woman's cries that she had to be removed from the courtroom.

Nationally between 1868 and 1899, just before the period covered by this book, 525 people were hanged in 499 executions, some being multiple hangings. Out of all murders 26.5% occurred under the influence of alcohol. The number of wife killings – uxoricide – was 122; 41% of the husbands were drunk when they killed their wives. None of the 15 murderesses, however, were drunk when they committed murder. They were motivated by such things as jealously or to claim insurance money.

Firearms were the most common means to kill, followed by slitting with knives, battering with a blunt instrument and stabbing with knives. Other methods included bludgeoning with axes, physical beatings, strangulation and poisoning. (*The Hangman's Record, Volume I, 1868–1899*, by Steve Fielding.)

A Chinatown Shooting

On 20 March 1904, in a lodging house inhabited by Chinamen at 22A Frederick Street, John Go Hing, a laundry keeper of New Chester Road, Rock Ferry, was shot to death by a man called Pong Lun. The shooting resulted from the game of Chinese dominoes, Mah Jong.

Four Chinamen were playing dominoes: Ah Foo, Moy Lee, a sailor, and the murdered man, Go Hing. Pong Lun entered the room. Ah Foo withdrew from the game and Moy Chung took his place. Four men only were able to play at once unless the banker agreed that more could take part. Go Hing was the banker. The sailor staked money and Pong Lun said he wanted to stake something. Go Hing owed Pong Lun about £3 and had paid him £1. Pong Lun took up a position behind the player Moy Chung. It was the rule that anyone outside the game could bet with the consent of the banker. Pong Lun wanted to back Moy Chung's hand but Go Hing refused to accept the bet. Pong Lun laid some chips or counters on the table, but Go Hing refused, saying that he had no bet with him. Some mention was made of the old standing debt between the two men, after which Pong Lun went out of the room and walked up and down in the kitchen.

Pong Lun went upstairs and afterwards returned and again stood behind Moy Chung. Go Hing again refused to pay him any winnings. Two revolver shots then rang out. Go Hing put his hand to his stomach and fell to the floor saying: 'Pong Lun has shot me.' Pong Lun left the room and two shots were heard outside, apparently being fired to deter anyone from following. Pong Lun then escaped from the house. A policeman was summoned, and Go Hing was removed to the Northern Hospital, suffering from a bullet in the abdomen near to his heart. He died of peritonitis on 23 March.

Pong Lun returned to the house on the night of the shooting and said the police could do what they liked. When arrested, he said: 'He owes me some money. I ask him for it and he say he pay me no more.' Keys were found on Pong Lun, one of which fitted a box in his bedroom. In the box were found some cartridges which fitted the five-chambered revolver. In the weapon were four discharged cartridges and one undischarged.

For the defence, Mr Madden said that Pong Lun would not be giving evidence because of his poor knowledge of English. He had been drinking whisky from 1.30 to 9.00 p.m. and had 'but the haziest idea of what had occurred'. Pong Lun was found guilty of murder and sentenced to death. The execution date was fixed for Tuesday 31 May, the same as for Kirwan in the Great Newton Street case. At 8.00 a.m. that morning, the double hanging was carried out at Walton Prison. Chaplain Rev. Morris told the *Liverpool Courier* that both men walked calmly to the scaffold and 'met their end stoically'. They seemed to listen to the words of the minister and seemed to be perfectly resigned to their fate. It was said that the pinioning of the condemned men was performed by hangman Billington 'with his usual tact and despatch'. Both men submitted without resistance.

Chinese Liverpudlians

Liverpool, it is commonly said, has one of the oldest Chinese communities in Europe. Chinese sailors arrived in Liverpool in the mid-nineteenth century after local shipping lines, such as The Ocean Steamship Company, began to sail to and from China. Inevitably, as with African seamen, some settled in Liverpool and married local women. The Chinese community grew up in the areas of Pitt Street and Cleveland Square, Liverpool's 'Chinatown'. Chinese seamen were paid at lower rates than British, regardless of whether they signed on in China or in a British port. Other forms of employment were therefore more attractive: boarding houses, laundries, grocery shops and restaurants provided alternatives to work at sea. A close-knit and largely self-sufficient community grew and developed in the early years of the twentieth century.

In contrast to the two cases involving Chinese men in this volume, Chinamen on the whole were not generally associated with violent or drunken behaviour. Research into the community carried out in 1906 reported that wives of Chinese men regarded their husbands to be kinder and more considerate than local British men. It was acknowledged that Chinese men were clean, hard-working and made good family men. The Chinese were associated, however, with a love of gambling. The gambling houses were more welcoming places to Chinese than the theatre or Music Hall, where they could be subjected to hostility or racist behaviour. Although the Chinese were not as harshly viewed by the authorities as the Black population they were still subject to the usual fears of host populations: lack of morality, the taking of jobs, influence on local women and opium smoking – all aspects of the so-called 'Yellow Peril'.

A Liverpool Hotel

Our story centres upon 29-year-old Allan Muir and his lover Isabella Mackenzie. Muir was a married man with a wife and children living in Bootle. He did not get on with his wife, however, because, it was suggested, of his drinking habits. Muir left his wife and followed the sea. He was second steward on board the Allan Line steamer *Pretorian*, trading between Glasgow and Canada. Muir's lover Isabella was Scottish and in 1898, a year after her marriage, she left her husband who was a trades-man in Glasgow. For the previous four or five years she had worked as a stewardess aboard *Pretorian*.

On 21 August 1904, *Pretorian* arrived in Glasgow and Mrs Mackenzie went home to her father's house. The following day she signed off the ship's articles and on the 23rd she left home. Her father never saw her again. On 4 September, Muir and Mackenzie drove up in a cab at the New Waverley Hotel in Lord Nelson Street, Liverpool. Muir asked for a room for himself and his wife. On 8 September, the couple took a cab to Muir's real wife's house in Bootle. There was a noisy disturbance between the Muirs which continued in the street where Isabella sat and waited in the cab. The police had to step in to sort out the scene of domestic disorder. Afterwards, Muir and Mackenzie drove back to their hotel, where they arrived at about midnight.

Two days later, the couple went out together after breakfast. From several chemists in and around Lime Street, they bought some potentially dangerous drugs – tincture of opium and belladonna liniment. On the morning of the 11th (a Sunday) hotel waitress Bridget White passed the lovers' room several times, but did not knock on their door. Bridget's suspicions were aroused when she had heard no sound from the room all day. At 7.00 p.m. she reported the matter to the proprietress of the Waverley, Mary Jane Byrne. Miss Byrne told Bridget to go up and see just what was going on. Bridget knocked at the door and got no reply. When the room was entered, Isabella Mackenzie and Allan Muir were lying in bed. Muir was breathing heavily and making a snoring noise. Isabella was silent.

The police were called in and found that Isabella was dead. Muir was very ill but he was made to get up and walk about until the ambulance arrived to take him to the Royal Infirmary. At the infirmary, a young doc-tor, Dr R. G. Willis, a house surgeon, saw Muir and thought he was suffering from alcoholic delirium tremens. Muir was then taken to the

Brownlow Hill Workhouse Hospital, where Dr Bligh diagnosed opium poisoning. Found in the hotel room were several letters which showed that a suicide pact had been agreed between Muir and Mackenzie.

As the law stood at that time, where two people agreed together to commit suicide and death took only one of them, the survivor was deemed guilty of murder. So it was that when Muir was discharged from hospital he was charged with the capital offence. When charged, he said to Detective Sergeant Pierrepoint: 'I did not kill her. We both agreed to die together. She went out and bought the stuff and we took equal amounts.'

On Monday 5 December 1904 Allan Muir appeared at St George's Hall charged with attempting to commit suicide at Liverpool on 11 September by taking poison, and of the wilful murder of Isabella Mackenzie on the same date. Muir was required to plead to the murder charge. He pleaded not guilty.

Two of the suicide letters found in the hotel room were read out in court by prosecuting counsel Mr Maxwell. The first was by Mackenzie, addressed to 'My Darling Little Children'. The other letter was from Muir to Mrs Muir. It read: 'I know not what to call you. I can't find words strong enough. You have ruined my life with your tongue. You have driven me to this. May God forgive me! He knows I had no love to show you. I know He will forgive me. I sincerely hope the dear little children will not take after you. You are the talk of everyone. Angel-woman you profess to be; you are bad to the core. May your soul be damned! You have ruined my life and the life of one who loves me, which you never did. Bless my children – Allan.'

The defence case was presented by Mr Riley. Two witnesses testified that Isabella Mackenzie was taking opium in 1901 and 1902. These were a ship's steward called Gray and a Glasgow woman called Christina Bonner. In his final address to the jury, Mr Riley said: 'It is probable that the taking of drugs would have led to her death one day. Even if Muir was a thousand miles from her, Mackenzie may have accidentally taken an overdose and Muir, in terror, may have decided to take his own life too. This was not murder.' Mr Riley's speech lasted for an hour and forty minutes.

Referring to the cause of Mrs Mackenzie's death, the judge, in his summing-up, said the idea that she had died by accident was destroyed by a letter she wrote to her father, begging for his forgiveness. The jury returned a 'guilty' verdict, with a strong recommendation to mercy. The judge delivered the mandatory death sentence to Muir and added that the sentence of the law should be set aside and a period of penal servitude given. On Sunday 11 December a reprieve for Muir was communicated from the Home Office to the authorities in Walton Prison.

The showing of mercy to commute a death sentence was, in past centuries, the prerogative of the Sovereign. This power to commute sentences was gradually delegated by the crown to judges and to the Home Secretary, a system first implemented in the provinces then extended to the London courts.

If the judge in a capital case was not satisfied that it merited the death sentence, he would first pronounce it in order to terrify the prisoner in the dock and bring home to him or her the gravity of their crime (after 1861 the pronouncement was in fact made compulsory). Then later either the judge or the Home Secretary might issue a reprieve and commute the death sentence.

Another Case of Poisoning in St Helens

On Thursday 8 December 1904 at St George's Hall, before Mr Justice Phillimore and a jury, there came to trial 49-year-old Ellen Burndred, charged with the murder by poison of a 15-year-old girl called Sarah Ann Jones.

At the age of six, Sarah was deserted by her father and was taken in by the workhouse at Whiston. She stayed there for six years. At that time, Ellen Burndred and her husband, a collier, together with a 14-year-old daughter called Sophia, were living in St Helens. In August 1901 Mrs Burndred applied to the authorities at the workhouse for a young girl to come and live with them as a companion for Sophia. That month, the child Sarah Anne Jones went to live there. Shortly after her arrival in the Burndred household, Sarah was insured with the Royal London Friendly Society for £20 at a premium of twopence a week.

From 1901 to 1904, Sarah was under the supervision of the Poor Law relieving officer of the district. He regularly visited the Burndred house and saw that the girl was in good health and apparently happy and contented. In February 1904 Mrs Burndred insured the child with the British Workman's General Insurance Society for £9, payable at one penny a week.

That same month, Mrs Burndred went to the workhouse and asked the officials if they would take the child back. She said Sarah had been disobedient and that she did not want to look after her any longer. Mrs Burndred was asked to reconsider her decision and she went back home, taking the child with her. However, on 21 April she took Sarah back to the workhouse. The very next day, the 22nd, Mrs Burndred applied for the child again, but she was refused. Sarah was not allowed back with the Burndreds until 2 July.

In May or June of 1904, Mrs Burndred visited the St Helens glassworks and asked a man there to supply her with some arsenic. She said she wanted it to lime-wash her house to prevent infestation by beetles. Her request was refused and she went home empty-handed.

On 25 July there was living with Mrs Burndred her husband, her daughter, a young male lodger, and Sarah Ann Jones. The dinner that day was prepared by Mrs Burndred. After the dinner had been eaten, Sarah and the young man were taken ill with stomach pains and diarrhoea. The lodger recovered but Sarah got worse. On 29 July, a Dr Bellew was called in and diagnosed gastritis. Up until her illness, Sarah slept in the same room as Sophia, but afterwards slept with Mrs Burndred. She grew worse, and on 7 August, she died.

After the death, Mrs Burndred applied for and got the insurance money, altogether about £29. The child was buried on 11 August, the funeral expenses being paid by Mrs Burndred. However, the coroner had the body exhumed and arsenic oxide crystals were found in the stomach, liver, kidneys and brain.

At her trial, the prosecution alleged that Mrs Burndred had been hard pressed for cash, as her husband was out of work and she was being pursued by numerous creditors. She had decided to dispose of Sarah in order to collect her life insurance money. On 21 August, Mrs Burndred was spotted near a local pond, throwing something into it. Later she was herself seen struggling in the pond and was rescued by a local man who witnessed her plight.

There was very strong circumstantial evidence against Ellen Burndred. One important point in her favour, though was that no arsenic was found in her house. In his defence case, Mr Riley emphasised this and mentioned the possibility of Sarah having eaten contaminated food. There had been many cases of arsenic contamination and the serving of arsenical beer had been so widespread that a Royal Commission had been set up to investigate the matter.

At the completion of his summing up, Mr Justice Phillimore, having gone over the evidence, said this to the jury: 'the child undoubtedly took arsenic. If she got it from contaminated food, there is no criminal responsibility on the part of the prisoner. If, by accident, Dr Bellew mixed arsenic in his medicine, he ought to be indicted for manslaughter. If there is any fair or reasonable explanation of this woman's conduct, or if you think her conduct has been so good that she could not do a think like this, you must find her not guilty, but in the event of you finding otherwise, you must return a verdict against her.'

The verdict was 'not guilty'. Mrs Burndred showed no sign of either relief or surprise. When the judge pronounced her discharge she stepped quietly from the bar and joined her husband and her friends who were seated at the back of the dock. The trial ended on the afternoon of the second day.

⁓ 1905 ⁓

Liverpool Liner Tragedy

Trials relating to serious offences committed aboard merchant vessels registered at Liverpool were heard at the Liverpool Assizes. On Monday 20 February 1905, Emil Baumann, a German sailor, appeared before Mr Justice Wills indicted with the wilful murder of William Maguire aboard the Booth liner *Cearenae* on 8 January on a voyage from Barbados to New York. There had been a hearing in New York after which Baumann had been extradited from America to face trial at Liverpool.

Baumann and Maguire were trimmers aboard the *Cearenae*. It was part of their duty to leave sufficient coal on the stoke plate to last the trimmers coming on duty for half an hour, while they cleaned out the furnaces and got rid of the ashes. On 8 January, Baumann was on duty from 12.00 to 4.00 p.m. and he was relieved by Maguire. When Maguire came on duty at 4.00 p.m. he noticed that Baumann had left hardly any coal on the stoke plate. He tackled Baumann about this, saying to the German: 'How is it you left so little coal?' There was a fairly heated exchange of words between the two men, with Baumann saying to Maguire, 'There is plenty – as much as I got,' before walking away. Some twenty minutes later, Baumann was seen upon the grating over the stoke hole. Maguire called to him to send down more coal. Baumann, who spoke broken English, was not pleased with Maguire's request. He called Maguire a filthy name and then added: 'Do you want to fight me? Me kill you!'

Baumann went into the forecastle and Maguire followed him. A man called James Mackay witnessed the ensuing events. 'When Maguire came into the forecastle after Baumann, the two men began to argue with each other. Finally, Maguire let out a cry of pain and blood began to gush from his chest. Mackay said that Maguire had no weapon and struck no blow at Baumann. The ship's doctor was called and found that Maguire had sustained two serious wounds – one in the chest and one in the abdomen. Within minutes, Maguire was dead.

It has been noted that certain trades increased the chances of facing the hangman's noose. Labourers, colliers, soldiers and sailors were highly represented in the numbers of the executed. The equipment used in these trades was, of course, potentially dangerous and always to hand.

At his trial, Baumann was defended by Mr Cuthbert Smith, who handed in a statement made by Baumann at the New York inquiry. He mentioned the quarrel having arisen between himself and Maguire in the stoke hole. Baumann said he then went upstairs into the forecastle. Shortly afterwards, he said, Maguire came in with an open knife in his hand and had struck him on the head with the handle of the knife. Baumann sank to the floor and Maguire kept hitting him. According to Baumann, Maguire said, 'I will kill you' and jumped upon him. Baumann said he really thought that Maguire would have killed him. Baumann denied threatening to kill Maguire. The report that he did so was, said Baumann, a lie. Mr Smith urged the jury to say that Baumann had acted without premeditation, that Maguire was the real assailant and that, if anything, Baumann was guilty of manslaughter.

The jury, who were out from 3.00 p.m. until 3.40 p.m., brought in a verdict of manslaughter. Mr Justice Wills said the crime had come very near to murder, and sentenced Baumann to penal servitude for sixteen years.

⋘⊙⊙⊙⋙

Birkenhead Murder Case at Old Priory

On Thursday 20 July 1905 at Chester Castle Assize Court, before Mr Justice Channell, there opened the trial of 36-year-old William Alfred Hancocks, a sheriff's officer who had lost an arm some years previously, for the murder of his 15-year-old daughter Mary Elizabeth Hancocks, a domestic servant, on 23 March 1905.

Hancocks, his wife and two little children aged 4 and 5, occupied one room in a house at 7 Old Priory in Birkenhead. Mary lived away from home and worked in Birkenhead for a draper called Evans. The girl often visited her parents when she had time off and it was while on one of these visits that Hancocks was alleged to have killed her.

On 23 March, Hancocks left the house in the morning and was out all day. That evening, at about 7.00 p.m., Mary came home to see her parents and went upstairs to their room. Hancocks returned home about 7.00 p.m. and Mrs Hancocks left the house to go shopping. Shortly afterwards, a neighbour called Mrs Storey, who was in the house at the time, heard Mary shout out 'Mrs Storey! Mrs Storey!' She immediately went upstairs, accompanied by Mrs Hancocks, who had just returned. When they got onto the landing they were joined by a third woman, a Mrs Wiley. The three of them entered Hancock's room. They found him and his daughter lying on a bed. Enraged by what she saw, Mrs Hancocks had words with her husband, at which Hancocks rushed at his wife with a knife, saying he would kill her, but Mrs Storey intervened and Mrs Hancocks and Mrs Wiley took refuge in another room. Mrs Storey got a policeman to Hancocks, who had apparently been drinking. For a few moments at least, peace was restored. Mary wanted to go back to her work, but Hancocks directed her to go back to their room and he followed.

In the meantime, Mrs Hancocks had left the house. Mrs Storey stood for a while at the front door and then went up to Mrs Wiley's room. When the two women had been there for about five minutes they heard Mary cry out. On hearing her cries, Mrs Storey went out for another policeman while Mrs Wiley went to Hancocks's room. Hancocks came running from the house in the direction of Woodside Ferry, followed by Mrs Storey's husband Samuel. Mary was found at the top of the staircase. She was unconscious and bleeding from a large wound on the left temple. Her hair and clothing were saturated with blood, and there was a large pool of blood near her head. There was a cut across her left wrist.

A chemist was sent for and he helped as much as he could before an ambulance was sent for. As it was about to leave for the hospital, orders were received for the ambulance to call at Woodside Ferry to pick up Hancocks, who had been fished out of the Mersey, so Father and daughter were conveyed to the hospital in the same van. There it was found that the girl had a severe head wound, the skull having been fractured. An operation was performed but she died a week later. A pocket-knife covered in blood was found in the room where the struggle had occurred. When Hancocks was first charged with attacking his daughter he said he knew nothing about it. Later, when asked about her condition, he said: 'I must have been mad when I did it; I thought such a lot of her.'

Constable Yates gave testimony that he was called to a disturbance and found that Hancocks, although he had been drinking, seemed to know what he was talking about. When Yates left the house he did not believe Hancocks presented any danger. Samuel Storey described how he ran after Hancocks down to Woodside. When he was near to Woodside Ferry Hotel, Hancocks turned round and shouted out to him: 'Keep off or I'll put something into you'.

Evan Green, a marine engineer, and Police Constable Willoughby gave evidence about Hancocks being rescued from the river. He was unconscious and was removed to hospital, where a few days later, before Mary was dead, Willoughby charged him with the attempted murder of his daughter. Hancocks replied: 'I don't remember anything at all about it.' After the death, when charged with murder, he stated that: 'All I can say is this: "I don't remember", and I don't remember'.

Evidence was given by Detective Sergeant Mountfield that on 5 April, with Constable Hughes, he went to Walton Gaol to bring Hancocks over to Birkenhead for a court appearance. Hancocks asked when they had buried his daughter and Mountfield replied 'On Monday'. Hancocks said: 'The wife is the cause of it. She is always harping at me for money and she caused me to break teetotal.' Mountfield warned Hancocks to remain silent but Hancocks went on to say: 'I will say nothing. I don't care if I hang but I would like to live for the children's sake, and if I get out of this I will never touch drink again.'

Evidence from a doctor suggested that if a man lost an arm in a railway accident, as Hancocks had done, it would cause a shock to the nervous system, but the effects would not last for more than two years. This evidence was called to prove Hancock's sanity.

In his remarks in defence of Hancocks, Mr Montgomery drew the attention of the jury to the fondness Hancocks had for the dead girl. He suggested that the girl may have lain down upon the bed as it was a quiet spot to rest and Hancocks, while standing near the bed, may have suddenly turned round to the girl, perhaps to speak to her, and being rather more drunk than had been suggested, Hancocks, with his one arm, could have stumbled heavily with the knife in his hand, across the girl and caused one of the wounds. In struggling, the girl would have received the cuts on her arm. Mr Montgomery said that Hancocks' inability to remember the offence was a memory lapse, just like the lapse he had when he was found wandering about carrying his severed arm, not knowing what had taken place.

The judge, who began his summing up at 1.15 p.m., said at the outset that he was sorry to say he could see nothing in the facts which would justify the jury in finding a verdict of manslaughter rather than murder. The jury, after half an hour's retirement, found Hancocks guilty, with a recommendation to mercy.

Mr Justice Channell pronounced sentence of death, after which Hancocks chirpily said 'Thank you, my lord', saluted the judge and was taken below. On hearing the sentence, Mrs Hancocks, sitting near the dock, fainted and had to be carried out.

On Friday 4 August 1905 a petition for reprieve was presented to the Home Secretary by representatives of Hancocks's solicitor, G. F. Lees. Two days later, the High Sheriff of Cheshire received a letter rejecting a reprieve. The execution was to go ahead on Wednesday 9 August at Knutsford Prison.

Alfred Hancocks was hanged at Knutsford at 8.00 a.m. The executioner was Billington assisted by Pierrepoint. The latter had devised a special device to enable Hancocks's single arm to be pinioned behind his back in the usual way. The execution was only the fifth to have taken place at Knutsford, the last one since August 1890.

Hancocks slept the previous night from 9.00 p.m. to 5.00 a.m. For his breakfast he had tea and bread and butter. He smoked his pipe afterwards. He walked the short distance to the scaffold firmly, with just the trace of a smile upon his lips, showing no sign of fear he toed the chalk mark on the scaffold calmly, and said nothing before the lever was pulled as the clock chimed eight. Death was instantaneous he made no struggle. It transpired that Hancocks had two wives to both of whom he left letters. He had married bigamously a woman named Bennett, seven or eight years earlier at Bristol, and his lawful wife having left him at Birmingham a little time before. She rejoined him at Birkenhead in 1899 and knew nothing of the bigamous union. The second wife, with her two children, was living in a Bristol workhouse.

On the morning of an execution the prisoner would be visited by the chaplain and then have breakfast. He would be moved to the holding cell near to the scaffold and here receive any sacraments or religious blessing if desired. Five minutes before the hour of execution the hangman would enter the cell, shake hands with the prisoner and then pinion the arms. A procession was then formed: the chief warder at the head, chaplain, prisoner and hangman (sometimes with an assistant). Flanking them would be eight warders, four on each side, and bringing up the rear was the governor or sheriff, two wand bearers and finally the prison surgeon. The chaplain would recite the Litany for the Dying, the hangman would adjust the noose and secure the prisoner's legs. Two warders stood at either side in case the prisoner collapsed. Then the lever was pulled. Also present were official witnesses, including members of the press.

An Everton Tragedy

On Friday 8 September 1905, Mr T. E. Sampson, Liverpool City Coroner, opened an inquest into the death of 52-year-old Eliza Jane West, the wife of John West of 1 Lorraine Street. West had been arrested on suspicion of having caused his wife's death. He was present in the coroner's court.

Testimony was given by the West's daughter, Mrs Harriet Baker. She said she lived with her parents in Lorraine Street and said that for the past five years her mother had been very much addicted to drink. During the three months or more before her death, Mrs West had been drunk nearly every day. She was a very quarrelsome person and this had been made worse by her heavy drinking. Mrs Baker said her father often came home to find no meal ready for him. Her mother used to antagonise her father but, said Mrs Baker, he never ill-treated her.

Mrs Baker described how, on 26 August (a Saturday) her mother was very drunk indeed. She threw her fish tea into the fire with the remark that the father was going to have no tea that day. Mrs Baker saw her father throw a knife across the table. Mrs West, standing near the dresser, cried out and put her hand to her left armpit. She began to bleed, so badly that she had to be taken to Stanley Hospital by ambulance.

Alfred Olsen, Mrs West's son-in-law, testified about something John West had said to him by way of explanation when he was on bail. According to Olsen, West said: 'She was aggravating me and I said,

'For God's sake shut up', and at the same time I threw the knife across the table onto the dresser where she was standing. She took the knife up in her hand and said, 'I will give you this if you talk to me like that'. She shook the knife at me. I told her to put it down and she refused, and I went to her and got hold of her right wrist. She turned round and put the knife under her cape and stooped down over the dresser. I put my hand over her shoulder to get the knife from her and with that she threw the knife on the dresser.

The inquest ended with the jury giving an 'open' verdict. They were unable to decide whether or not Mrs West was stabbed deliberately or by accident, but John West was detained in custody. On 21 September, after a hearing of the evidence against him, he was committed to stand trial for murder at the forthcoming Winter Assizes.

West's trial was held on Monday 4 December 1905. As befitted his employment as a clerk, 53-year-old West wore a smart dark suit. After the prosecution witnesses had given their evidence, the judge, Mr Justice Ridley, said: 'There is no evidence here on which it would be right to convict of murder. That charge had better be withdrawn from the jury. It will now be a charge of manslaughter.' Mr Riley, defending, said Mrs West's fatal wound was not caused by a knife being thrown, but during a struggle. The judge said that in that case the jury ought to acquit West. Without leaving their box, the jury gave a 'not guilty' verdict and applause broke out in court when the verdict was declared. John West was then released.

Toxteth Dock

On Tuesday 10 October 1905, William Edward Hitchen, 28, who was living in an apartment at 12 Helmingham Road, off Hinderton Road in Tranmere, appeared in the Dale Street Police Court on a murder charge. The previous night, a 24-year-old man called Thomas Williams, a dock board timekeeper, was knocked over the river wall at Toxteth Dock, and fell to his death in the Mersey. William's body was recovered after an hour in the river and taken to the Southern Hospital by horse ambulance. Unfortunately, the hospital staff could not revive him.

Thomas Williams was lodging with a Mrs Sarah Ann Snell at 351 Park Road in Liverpool. He could not swim but was learning to do so. The river wall of the dock had a narrow gauge railway running on the top of it, about two feet from the edge, and at the time Williams fell into the river, the water was twelve feet deep and 24 feet from the top of the wall. William's funeral took place at Smithdown Road Cemetery after a service by the Rev. J. E. Haughton at St Gabriel's, Toxteth.

An inquest into the affair opened on Wednesday 18 October 1905. Several witnesses' evidence helped to piece together the events leading up to William's fate. Thomas Moore, the driver of a stationary engine employed by the dock board on underpinning work on the Toxteth Dock river wall, said he worked with Hitchen, who was his fireman, stoking the engine. Moore said that they started night duty together at 6.00 p.m. and he noticed Hitchen had been drinking. Moore let Hitchen go away from the engine at 6.45 p.m. and he returned at 9.45 p.m. At ten they both knocked off for supper and went to a nearby pub where Hitchen drank one and a half pints of beer. Moore went back to his work at 10.30 p.m., but Hitchen did not return until 11.10 p.m. when he was clearly drunk. He went to the engine house. Williams left the engine house shortly afterwards and Hitchen followed him.

A few minutes later, Hitchen said to Moore: 'I have put the timekeeper into the river.' Moore testified that he didn't think Hitchen was serious and ignored the remark. Hitchen went away again, and then a man called Mayer came and told Moore that Hitchen really had pushed Williams into the Mersey.

James Silcock, a carpenter's labourer, said he was standing opposite the engine house at 11.10 p.m. Hitchen came up to Silcock and asked him where the timekeeper was. Silcock told Hitchen that the timekeeper was in his hut and Hitchen went in that direction. After a few minutes, Williams walked past with Hitchen a few feet behind.

Labourer James Murray saw the two men pass by him. Hitchen was about a yard and a half behind Williams and as Hitchen passed, he said: 'I will do for that fellow tonight, Murray.' Murray followed them. He saw Hitchen and Williams standing face to face, Williams with his hands in his pockets, and his back to the river. They were talking. Hitchen drew back his two hands and hit Williams on the chest. It was not a violent blow, but Williams fell backwards over the river wall and into the river, turning two somersaults as he fell. Moore got a rope and threw it to Williams, who was struggling in the water, but before Williams could reach it he sank and did not reappear. The alarm was sounded and a boat lowered but the body was not found until 2.00 a.m.

Mayer and another man described how they heard Hitchen say to Williams: 'Are you going to book me on?' Williams replied: 'No, not at this time. You are over half an hour behind your time.' Hitchen persisted, saying to Williams: 'So you are not going to book me on, then?' 'No', said Williams, 'I have told you I won't.' Hitchen followed Williams to the far side of the crane and Williams again refused. Then Hitchen hit Williams clean off his feet and over the wall. He said to Mayer: 'You don't say anything more about it.'

A man called Archie Trench described how he saw Hitchen putting on his boots in the engine house. Trench said to him: 'How are you now, Billy?' Hitchen replied: 'That timekeeper wouldn't book me on, but he's all right now. He is in the river, where he ought to be.' Hitchen was arrested at Tranmere at 3.00 a.m. on the Tuesday morning. He said: 'Is he dead?' When he heard that Williams was indeed dead Hitchen said: 'I am very sorry.'

Hitchen was tried at St George's Hall on Friday 1 December. In his sum-ming up, Mr Justice Ridley said to the jury:

> The question of drink may be taken into account when there has been provo-cation, but in this case there has been no provocation. People must clearly understand that in no case can intoxication be relied upon as lessening the offence. If the jury thinks that, whatever precise degree of drunkenness the prisoner had reached, he had made up his mind to put the deceased into the river, and that he did it accordingly, they ought to convict him on the capital charge.

The jury were out considering their verdict between 2.00 and 2.45 p.m. They found Bill Hitchen guilty of wilful murder with a very strong recom-mendation to mercy on account of his drunkenness and the shortness of pre-meditation. Sentence of death was then pronounced by the judge. Throughout the trial, Hitchen seemed to feel his position acutely. He sat with bowed head during the whole of the evidence, and while his counsel and the judge addressed the jury he remained with his head buried in his hands, apparently in tears. After sentence of death had been passed, Hitchen fainted and was carried from the dock unconscious.

A petition for reprieve of the death sentence, containing some 26,000 signatures, was sent to the Home Secretary by solicitor John Bateman of 115A Dale Street. On 15 December 1905, a reprieve was granted. Hitchen's sentence was commuted to penal servitude for life.

Petitioning was a means by which the relatives of a condemned prisoner and the general public could appeal for mercy. This became a popular form of 'people power' from the early nineteenth century onwards.

Raleigh Street

On the afternoon of Monday 11 December 1905, between 4.00 and 5.00 p.m., a clothing and general dealer by the name of David Morris Cohen was standing outside his shop in Derby Road, Bootle, when a drunken man approached him. It was John Hughes, a 43-year-old dock labourer. Hughes drew from his pocket a sailor's knife in a sheath and said to Cohen: 'I am going to commit a murder with this before I am finished.' Keeping his nerve, Cohen told him, 'You wouldn't kill a fly'. Hughes then said: 'Yes I love her but she is a bitch,' and staggered onwards along Derby Road. Hughes then made his way to a registered common lodging house at 36 Raleigh Street where he lived with Catherine, his wife of some twenty years, in a back room on the first floor. As soon as Hughes got into the house, he went to his bed.

Between 9.00 and 10.00 p.m. that night, the landlady of the lodging house, a Mrs Cahill, was in her kitchen, immediately below the room occupied by John and Catherine Hughes. She heard something fall on the floor above with a loud thud. A woman in the room next to the Hugheses heard what she later described as 'a sort of scuffle and a slash on the floor'. Mrs Cahill shouted up to Hughes: 'Jack, do you think nobody pays any rent in the house but you?' Hughes put his head out of the room and said: 'Goodnight ma, I'm going to bed. God bless you.'

At about 10.00 p.m. a woman who was living with her parents in the next house happened to go into the yard. She recognised Catherine Hughes's voice calling out, 'Oh, Jack don't!' Other women, living in the back attic of a house two doors away heard Catherine scream: 'Jack, don't kill me!' and 'Don't get the knife to me!' The argument between the couple seemed to have arisen over Mrs Hughes pawning a pair of her husband's boots.

During the course of the argument over the boots, Mrs Hughes was stabbed in the stomach. On the morning after the stabbing, the injured Catherine went downstairs to the yard of the house to get a drink of water. Later in the day she showed the wound to two women who were staying at the house. On the Wednesday, the 13th, Dr Sanders was called on by a district nurse, but he was not told of the stab wound, and he prescribed for bronchitis, from which Mrs Hughes was also suffering.

On the Thursday, Hughes told Mrs Cahill, 'Kate is dying. I am going for the priest'. Between 10.00 and 11.00 p.m., Dr Regan went to the house.

He saw the woman's wound, but did not dress it. At this point Hughes had already been put under arrest and Chief Inspector Leslie went to the house with Constable Smith. He took Hughes up to Kate's bedside and asked her how she got injured. Mrs Hughes replied that she and her husband had had 'a bit of a falling out' on Monday night, and that he had given her 'a bit of a dig in the stomach' with a knife. She died shortly afterwards, aged 42.

On the way to the Bridewell, Hughes was alleged to have said: 'I am afraid it is a case of this time. I didn't think she would round on me.' When charged with murder he replied 'Not guilty'. There was no trace of the sailor's knife, but two ordinary house knives were found in the room, one in the bedclothes.

An inquest into Kate Hughes's death was held at Bootle on Wednesday 20 December 1905. The inquest jury returned a verdict of wilful murder against Hughes. The case came to trial at the Liverpool Assizes before Mr Justice Grantham and a jury on 20 February 1906. Presenting the Crown's case against Hughes, Mr Kennedy described the events as 'a tale of penury and squalor'. He described the lodging house as 'a small house with a distressingly large number of people living in it'.

Mr Riley, defending Hughes, suggested to the jury that Mrs Hughes might have been injured by someone other than her husband. It was possible, he said, that she fell on the knife, or perhaps Hughes had fallen on top of her 'in the course of a drunken encounter'. At the worst, said Mr Riley, Hughes was guilty only of manslaughter.

Summing up, the judge said that no one else had caused the fatal injury. The jury had to decide if it had been caused wilfully or accidentally. The judge pointed out that the dead woman's face was covered with wounds and bruises. There was scarcely any natural skin left. Mr Justice Grantham said he had never heard of such a case before. Dr Pearson, who carried out a post mortem, said there was a stomach wound five or six inches deep, created by 'considerable violence' and ultimately causing death.

The jury left the room at 4.45 p.m. and returned with their verdict twelve minutes later. It was 'guilty of manslaughter'. In reply to the judge, Chief Inspector Leslie said that Hughes had thirty-six convictions – for drunkenness, wilful damage and assaulting the police. Once he had been convicted for stabbing his wife. Four months prior to the offence, said the inspector, he had scarcely been sober, and the wife was little better. Mr

Justice Grantham said that Hughes had 'lived a life not fit for a dog'. His relations with his wife were, said the judge, 'scarcely human'. He then went on to say: 'In Liverpool there is a great deal too much of this horrible brutality, drunkenness and the use of the knife'. He sentenced Hughes to fifteen years penal servitude.

Housing

In the late nineteenth century Liverpool Corporation was taking steps to tackle the poor quality of housing in the city. Acts passed between 1842 and 1864, including the 1864 Liverpool Sanitary Amendment Act, gave Liverpool extensive control of housing and made it a pioneer of housing reform. Unfortunately, the level of poor housing had built up before 1842 to such an extent that even by the 1950s there were still areas of housing which were in-sanitary, overcrowded and ridden with vermin. The rotten housing made life wretched for their occupants, many of whom had to deal with other problems such as periodic unemployment. It is not surprising that many of these occupants' lives could become nasty and brutish.

Liverpool grew rapidly from the late eighteenth century. To accommodate the growth in the city's trade and the numbers of people who came to the city to work on its expanding system of docks, houses were rapidly built near to the areas of work. The private firms who built them found it profitable and there were no restrictions or regulations for them to adhere to. The wealthy merchants left the city centre to live in the spacious and healthier suburbs, while their old houses were used to house several families and soon became overcrowded slums.

The majority of the working-class poor were housed in courts and their cellars. Courts were enclosed, dark, grim, airless and insanitary. The cellars, which were also used to accommodate families, were often damp and filthy and, if flooded during heavy rainfalls, became swamped with sewage; some inspections of the cellar dwellings reported that the local cess pit was leaking into them. It is little wonder that Dr Hope, the Medical Officer of

Health for Liverpool, referred to cellar dwellings as 'disease factories'. The death rate in Liverpool in May 1906 was recorded as 27 per 1000. It was also noted that the occupants of the courts and cellars turned to alcohol and its concomitants – crime and immorality. Pat O'Mara lived in court housing as a child and he gives a vivid description of one in Stanhope Street:

'... what the "Court" represented was a narrow alley receding off the street to a larger areaway, like an unseen tooth cavity, and ending in a conglomeration of filthy shacks. About twenty-five large families – dock labourers, hawkers, sooty artisans and their children – lived in the average court. Two revoltingly dirty toilets stood in the areaway and were always in demand; a queue usually waited in line, newspaper in hand. The shacks were so closely packed together and their walled partitions so thin that one had no choice but to listen to what went on on either side. Screams often rent the air at night, one courter waylaying another in the darkness. The cheaper elderly whores favoured the courts, and could always be found attending to their furtive business in the darker corners. Huge cats continually stalked the place, their eyes an eerie phosphorescence in the darkness.

✎ 1906 ✎

Anfield Cemetery

St George's Hall in Liverpool in May 1906 was the venue for the murder trial of John Hill, alias Rawsthorne, a 34-year-old shoeblack of no fixed address. He was alleged to have killed a 12-year-old boy called William Armitage in Anfield Cemetery on 10 March 1906.

At the outset of the trial before Mr Justice Bigham, defending counsel Mr Greaves Lord called a witness who suggested that Rawsthorne was unfit to plead to a charge of murder because he was of unsound mind. Dr Price, Medical Officer at Walton Gaol, said that Rawsthorne was 'mentally weak – a mental degenerate'. He would not be able to understand court evidence. He had responded to gaol discipline but appeared to have had no discipline all his life. The matter of Rawsthorne's sanity was put to the jury. They found him fit to plead and the trial went ahead. The prisoner, who had burst into tears while the question of his sanity was under discussion, pleaded not guilty.

On Saturday 10 March 1906 at about 1.15 p.m. the dead body of young William Armitage was found lying in a remote corner of a field which adjoined Anfield Cemetery. The body was still warm, and death must have occurred very shortly before – between 12.45 and 1.15 p.m. The cause of death was strangulation, using a handkerchief which had been fastened around the boy's neck. There was a wound in the neck, but that had not caused death.

William Armitage lived with his parents at 91 West Derby Road. His father, Richard Armitage, kept a small shop selling herbal beer. He was also employed at the Stanley Cattle Market and was a collector for a clothing society. Rawsthorne earned his living by shining people's shoes and by running errands. Small boys in the street used to make fun of him and irritated him by called him 'Johnny Raw' and 'Soft Johnny'. He often used to lose his temper with them.

Anfield Cemetery
Liverpool Record Office, Liverpool Libraries and Information Services

About 6 March, the boy Armitage and several other lads teased Rawsthorne in West Derby road and he chased them. On the evening of Friday 9 March, Rawsthorne went into Mr Armitage's shop while the boy was there. Mr Armitage noticed that his son seemed frightened of Rawsthorne, who whispered something to him. Next day, Mr Armitage sent William on messages in connection with his clothing club. To carry out his instructions, the boy would have had to go to Victoria Street and to Bodley Street in Walton. He got as far as Bodley Street some time in the afternoon of that day. On going out of a shop he said to someone unseen 'Come along'. About that time, Rawsthorne was spotted standing at the gates of Stanley Park, which was very close to Bodley Street. A boy dressed like Armitage was seen walking towards Rawsthorne. Other people saw the man and the boy walking down Walton Lane by the side of Stanley Park, and they were also seen at the boat pond in the park. One witness saw them going along the drive in Anfield Cemetery in the direction of the non-conformist chapel.

Beyond the chapel there was an outhouse, behind which was a field. At 12.55 p.m. on 10 March, a man named Carr, the owner of the field, saw Rawsthorne crossing the land and heading in the direction of Breck Road railway station. The man was coming from the corner in which the out-house of the cemetery was located. Because he was trespassing, Carr asked him what he was doing there. Rawsthorne replied: 'I am going to Breck Road station'. Carr said: 'You have no business here', at which Rawsthorne, chased by Carr's dog, ran away back towards the cemetery and made good his escape.

At 1.15 p.m. that afternoon, a labourer at the cemetery discovered the lifeless body of William Armitage in the field, close to the outhouse. The ground was soft, and there was what appeared to be the marks of a struggle having taken place. The boy was bleeding at the neck, around which a handkerchief was tightly tied.

Later in the afternoon of the killing, Rawsthorne was seen again in Walton Lane. At 4.00 p.m. he returned to the lodging house where he had been staying. When Rawsthorne was asked by a man called Thomas Burns if he had been to the football match he said he had. On the day of the boy's funeral, Rawsthorne encountered a woman in Mount Vernon Street and asked her: 'Are you going to the funeral?'

'What funeral?' asked the woman. Rawsthorne replied: 'The funeral of the little boy who was murdered in Anfield.' He went on to say: 'Look here, missus, if I had been ten minutes earlier I could have saved that boy's life. He was as warm as any of us standing here.'

On 20 March Rawsthorne was arrested in Kensington, Liverpool. The police officer noticed he was walking lame. He asked Rawsthorne what was the cause of it and Rawsthorne said: 'I scratched it with a rusty nail. I have been in Brownlow Hill workhouse for the last six weeks with it.' It was true that he had been in the workhouse, but he had been discharged on 5 March. Later on, Rawsthorne saw Inspector Foulkes at the Detective Office. He told the inspector he had not seen the boy since the Friday night when he saw him going into his father's shop. Trembling, Rawsthorne said: 'It's as bad as the Smithdown road murder (the unsolved killing of a little girl). The inspector asked him why he was trembling. 'I am cold and hungry', Rawsthorne replied.

In his speech to the jury, Mr Lord appealed to them to say that even if the prisoner did commit the crime, he was not capable of distinguishing the nature and quality of his actions. Mr Lord submitted that the verdict should be either manslaughter or, if the prisoner did commit murder, he was insane at the time.

In his summary, Mr Justice Bigham (later Lord Mersey) asked the jury to answer two questions. The first was: did the evidence satisfy them that it was the accused who killed the boy? The second question was: did he know at the time of the murder that he was doing wrong? After half an hour's consultation the jury returned a verdict of guilty with a strong

> *The sentence of the Court upon you is, that you be taken from this place to a lawful prison and thence to a place of execution and that you be hanged by the neck until you are dead; and that you body be afterwards buried within the precincts of the prison in which you shall be confined before your execution. And may the Lord have mercy on your soul. Amen.*

recommendation to mercy. Asked if he had anything to say, Rawsthorne replied: 'I was not there at all'. The condemned man sobbed violently as the judge passed the death sentence, compulsory for a murder conviction. He had to be helped down to the cells by warders. The judge said he would forward the jury's recommendation of mercy to the proper quarter, and would add a recommendation of his own.

On Monday 21 May 1906, acting on the recommendation of the jury supported by the trial judge, the Home Secretary reprieved Rawsthorne. His sentence was commuted to life imprisonment.

Sussex Street

Friday 3 August 1906 saw the opening, at St George's Hall, of the trial of Mrs Hannah Powell for the murder of her son John. On the bench was Mr Justice Kennedy. When Mrs Powell came into the dock she was crying bitterly, assisted up the stairs from the cells by two women warders. It was a minute or so before she managed to get herself fairly composed and able to listen to the indictment, read out by the clerk of the court. Mrs Powell kept her head steadily bent, with averted gaze, as she rocked herself to and fro. Prosecuting counsel Dr A. P. Thomas then stood up and began his opening remarks, outlining the case against Mrs Powell, who was 52.

Hannah Powell lived with her husband at 23 Sussex Street, off Park Road in the Dingle area of Liverpool. John Powell was eleven years of age, the son of Thomas Powell, a journeyman boilermaker. Also living in the house was a married daughter Emily and her husband, as well as a 14-year-old daughter, Christine Powell, sister of the dead boy.

Hannah Powell had got into the habit of having drunken binges. For the six weeks prior to the death of John Powell she had been drinking heavily, getting drunk nearly every day and eating little or no food. She began to complain of severe headaches and had become very nervous and overwrought. On Saturday night, 12 May 1906, Mrs Powell's daughter Emily found her drunk in the street. She was taken into the house and put to bed in her own bedroom, which was on the ground floor. Mr Powell and the other members of the household were all in their beds before midnight. John Powell and his sister Christine slept in the middle bedroom on the first floor. The door of this room was already off its hinges.

At about 7.30 a.m. on the Sunday, Christine was awakened by John, screaming out 'Oh! Oh!' several times. Looking up, the girl saw John kneeling on his bed. Blood was spurting from his throat and he fell back onto the bed. Christine ran upstairs to the next floor and woke her sister Mrs Brodie, who went downstairs and saw, lying on the staircase, past the room where the boy had been sleeping, a bloodstained razor. All the occupants of the house were roused by this time, but Mrs Powell was not in the house. She seems to have gone out into the street, where she spoke to a man called George Seddon. Mrs Powell said to him: 'Oh, George, can you find him? I have cut Johnny's throat.' She also said to a man called Bridson: 'Oh, Johnny, I have done it. I have cut Johnny's throat!' Bridson took Mrs Powell into his house and advised her to give herself up. Apparently referring to her husband, she said: 'He has been nagging at me all night.' She was also seen by Lucy O'Hare, to whom she said: 'Will you come with me to Essex Street? I want to give myself up. Johnny is dead.' Mrs O'Hare took Mrs Powell into a shop and bought her some ginger beer.

Bill Brodie, Mrs Powell's son-in-law, was awakened by shouts and screams from the floor below. Someone cried out: 'Johnny's throat's cut!' In a shop at the corner of Northumberland Street he found Hannah. She looked very excited and her whole body was trembling. She was drinking her ginger beer. Brodie said to her: 'What have you done?' At first she made no answer, but later she admitted: 'I have done it'.

'Done what?' asked Bridson.

'Done Johnny,' she replied.

When a policeman came on the scene, Mrs Powell gave herself up to him, saying 'I have cut my son's throat'. Young John was taken to the Royal

Southern Hospital but he was dead before he reached medical help; his jugular vein had been severed. At the bridewell, Mrs Powell admitted killing her son with the razor which was found on the staircase.

In court, the offending razor was passed around the jury for them to inspect. Mr Maxwell said: 'It may be suggested that the prisoner was not at the time responsible for her actions. No doubt the jury will give every consideration to that, as well as to all the facts.'

Dr Price, Chief Medical Officer at Walton Prison, said that Mrs Powell had been under his supervision since 14 May. When admitted, she was nervous and excited. She was very emotional and depressed from time to time, but 'not more than a person would be who realised the gravity of what she had done'. Dr Price said he had spoken with her daily and she had answered everything 'rationally and coherently'. Cross-examined by defence counsel Greaves Lord, Dr Price said that the loss of a child four years ago (a young daughter was burnt to death) might have caused 'melancholia and a liability to mental disease'. With an emotional woman like Mrs Powell, it was quite possible, said Mr Price, that the presence of drink would 'materially increase the liability to disease of the mind'. Dr Price went on: 'I should say that waking from a short drunken sleep might cause a disorder or derangement of the mind, which would render her permanently or temporarily unable to appreciate the nature of the act. Mrs Powell was not now suffering from any disease of the mind'. When in custody, she had said: 'If my husband had let me out this would not have happened.'

During his summing up, Mr Justice Kennedy said that 'She must have known what she was doing'. Here, Mrs Powell wept and moaned loudly. Later on, the judge said: 'I think everything connected with the case points to the fact that she was subject to slight attacks of melancholia.'

Mr Lord made an impassioned plea to the jury on Hannah Powell's behalf. He said: 'I ask the jury to say that this woman, although guilty of murder, was at the time she committed it, insane, and therefore she should not suffer the extreme penalty.' Mr Lord emphasised the fact that since the death of her child four years ago, she had been melancholy and depressed. He said: 'Flying to drink for solace, it had affected her mind. This was shown by her remark "I will be next". Every act from the moment she committed the crime was the act of a woman suffering from the most intense remorse. It might well be that the cry of the child, and the sight of the

The McNaughton Case and Rules

Daniel McNaughton (or McNaghten, there are different spellings of his surname in the records) was the illegitimate son of a Glasgow wood-turner. In January 1843 he shot the private secretary of the Prime Minister, Sir Robert Peel. Drummond, the man in question, died five days later. This was a case of mistaken identity, as McNaughton had wanted to kill the PM.

McNaughton had a history of eccentric behaviour and of claims that he was being persecuted by organisations and individuals. For example, one organisation he accused was the Catholic Church. He felt the Tories were persecuting him and the focus of his paranoia finally settled on the Tory PM, Peel, who had created the Metropolitan Police, another body that McNaughton had accused of persecuting him.

At his trial it was established that a person, who by all account appeared normal, rational and able to function within society, could also be partially insane and under delusions that would cause them to commit a criminal act. Under the McNaughton rules a person had to be deprived of awareness that what he or she was doing was wrong. This had to be a defect of reason as a result of a disease of the mind rather than actions undertaken because of ignorance, mistakes or because of differences of opinion.

Instead of being sent to the scaffold McNaughton was sent to Bethlem Hospital and after this to Broadmoor.

blood, had restored her to sanity, but at the time she committed the act she was not, I submit, mentally responsible.'

Applying the McNaghten rules as a test of insanity, the judge asked the jury to consider whether or not Mrs Powell understood the nature and quality of her lethal act, and whether she knew whether her act was wrong. Without leaving the box, the jury found that Mrs Powell was guilty of wilful murder, but that she was insane at the time she committed the act. Mr Justice Kennedy said: 'On that finding, I order the prisoner to be kept in custody as a criminal lunatic until His Majesty's pleasure shall be known.' Mrs Powell wept pitifully in the dock as the judge pronounced her fate.

~ 1907 ~

Another Portland Street Tragedy

On 6 May 1907, there opened the trial of Thomas Nolan, a dock labourer, charged with the murder of his wife. The crime was alleged to have been committed on Sunday 24 March in a cellar at 113 Portland Street, between Vauxhall Road and Scotland Road in Liverpool.

Nolan had been out of work for more than three years, largely, it was said, owing to his own dislike of employment. During those years he had been practically kept by his own wife's earnings from charring and cleaning. There was frequent quarrelling between the couple. From time to time their life together was made miserable by Nolan's outrageous conduct when under the influence of drink.

On Sunday 24 March, Mr and Mrs Nolan seemed to be on good terms. Mrs Nolan was last seen alive at 10.00 p.m. on that day. At 5.30 a.m. the following morning a knocker-up called Mrs McCormack, according to the arrangement, went to the cellar occupied by the couple in Portland Street and knocked on the door. She heard Nolan come to the door and say 'All right'. It was alleged that at the time Mrs McCormack called, Mrs Nolan was lying dead in the cellar.

At 11.15 p.m. that Monday, Nolan went to the main bridewell and told the officer on duty that he had murdered his wife with a hammer. On being asked for an explanation Nolan alleged that he was being 'persecuted by a club of men in Gerard Street', and that he 'did not like to leave his wife behind'. The police went to the cellar and found Mrs Nolan lying with her head battered by a hammer or some such instrument. The body had been cut and stabbed with a knife. The police made inquiries into Nolan's statements about the Gerard Street club, but they could not find any traces of such a club or group.

At the trial, which was held before Mr Justice Pickford, several witnesses described how, when in drink, Nolan tended to behave very strangely. He

Quite of a number of the cases in this volume have excessive drinking at the heart of them leading to murder. While drunkenness was not an excuse for murder, it was recognised that long-term excessive drinking could lead to either temporary or permanent insanity. The McNaughton rules would be cited in these cases.

It was important to establish whether a person had committed murder after losing their self-control when drunk, or whether they had decided they wished to kill a person beforehand and getting drunk to carry out the act. This was the difference between a conviction for manslaughter, and a sentence of penal servitude, and one of murder and an appointment with the hangman.

used to run up and downstairs talking to himself, very often quoting Shakespeare as he did so. One witness said he was 'a madman' when drunk. Some of the locals knew him as 'Crack Pot'. His sister was out of her mind and his father died in the asylum. Many times Nolan had threatened to take his wife's life.

The police sergeant at the bridewell, to whom Nolan surrendered himself, said that when he charged Nolan he replied: 'My mind has been driving wrong. I don't know what I am doing.' He added that he had been persecuted by a club. Police Constable Murray went to the cellar at Portland Street and found Mrs Nolan lying with her face covered by a pillow. She was dead. All her clothing was stained with blood. In the cellar, Murray found a hammer, a bloodstained table knife and a clasp knife, as well as a piece of paper on which Nolan had written a lengthy statement attempting to show that he had been 'shadowed' by certain men, who had subjected him to 'severe persecution'. Nolan also said that his home had been watched night and day. There was no sign of a struggle and it seemed that Mrs Nolan was asleep when she was attacked.

In evidence, Dr House said that when he saw Nolan the day after the killing, he believed he was suffering from the effects of chronic alcoholism. He regarded Nolan's talk about the club in Gerard Street as hallucination. Cross-examined by defence counsel Mr Segar, Dr House said that a man suffering from chronic alcoholism would be liable to lose his reason for an interval. The doctor said that Nolan's appearance on 25 March was 'consistent with his having been temporarily insane 24 hours previously'. Dr John Hay described Mrs Nolan's terrible wounds and agreed with Dr House that chronic alcoholism could give rise to an attack of temporary insanity.

Mr Segar asked the jury to say that Nolan was not responsible for his actions at the time he attacked his wife. The jury found Nolan 'guilty but insane'. The judge ordered Nolan's detention until His Majesty's pleasure be known. He remarked: 'The jury has taken a merciful view of this case'.

A Demented Mother

Three days after the Portland Street case was tried at St George's Hall, there came before Mr Justice Pickford the case of Louisa Cameron, 47, of 6 Vaughan Street, Liverpool. She was indicted for the murder of her son, Charles Cameron, aged nine years. Leading prosecuting counsel was the famous Liverpool barrister Mr F. E. Smith, later ennobled as Lord Birkenhead.

Mrs Cameron's husband was a labourer who was away working at Rhyl. He had not been home since Easter. The Camerons had several children, the eldest of whom was a son away in the Navy. Living at home were Herbert (15), Matilda (13) and the dead boy, Charles (9). Charles was 'mentally defective' and attended the Beacon Lane School for such handicapped children. Mrs Cameron had not been well for some time before the day of the tragedy and she was being treated for nervous debility by a local medical mission.

On 7 April 1907, Louisa Cameron complained to the mission doctor of pains in the head. She seemed very strange in her manner. During that same day, Herbert and Matilda were arguing and fighting with Charles when Mrs Cameron said to them: 'You will not have him long to hit. I'll get rid of him before I get rid of myself.'

On the morning of 9 April, Mrs Cameron received a letter from her son George at sea. It was written in a very unfriendly tone and it caused her some annoyance. Charles returned home from school that afternoon soon after

4.00 p.m. and at 5.00 p.m., a woman called Elizabeth Tull saw Mrs Cameron standing at her open door. Mrs Tull stopped and noticed that somebody was lying just inside the room. There was blood on Louisa Cameron's hands and on the floor. Mrs Tull asked her what she had done and she replied that she had killed her little boy. When asked why, Mrs Cameron replied: 'He asked for a butty and I had none. Poverty has done this.' Then the woman wailed: 'Let me die. I want to die now. I may as well do to myself what I have done to my child.' She later said she had been having trouble with her daughter who had been accused by the police of stealing a sovereign. What with that trouble and trouble with her husband, she did not know what she was doing.

Mrs Tull and a Mrs Donnelly went into the house, where they found the boy Charles lying in the kitchen with his throat cut. Two jugular veins had been completely severed and he was stone dead. From the floor alongside the body, Mrs Donnelly picked up a bloodstained knife. The police were at once contacted and Mrs Cameron was arrested.

Young Herbert Cameron, in evidence, said his mother had been very fond of Charles. On the morning of 8 April she was very troubled after receiving a letter from George. The letter was written while cruising with the Channel fleet and it read;

I am sorry I cannot see you before my twentieth birthday, and when I see you I will have a full reckoning with you. When I come to look over my correspondence with you it makes my whole brain shake to think I have not a better home to go to. You encourage laziness and you ought to remain as you are. I have been considering the matter and have come to the conclusion that you have been a fool for years and years, although you could have been happy long ago. There is another brother out in India, another deserted home, and myself away from home. Your miserable career had not been going on for weeks and months, but for years. Don't be surprised if you hear I am married, because it would drive anyone insane. I am sick of hearing the same old news since I have been in the Navy. Please oblige me and don't write before I see you in August, and then perhaps you, on the twentieth birthday of my miserable life, will ask yourself some questions.

A policeman who was called to the house found Mrs Cameron standing by her son's lifeless body. As the policeman approached her, she cried out: 'Oh my child, what have I done?' When charged with murder, she said: 'I have been very low-spirited lately, what with the girl's trouble, the father being away from home, and I had a very nasty letter from my son, who is in the Navy, this morning.' The house was searched after the tragedy and Detective Sergeant Morrison found half of a two pound loaf, some butter and some fish in the oven. At the bridewell, there was found on Mrs Cameron after her arrest a half sovereign and 6½d.

After F. E. Smith had closed the case for the Crown, Mr Madden called into the witness box a Dr Smart. The doctor said that he examined Mrs Cameron on 28 April at Walton Gaol hospital wing. She was depressed and alcoholic, and she told him she had been worried by her family, her husband, and by lack of money and food. Mrs Cameron also told Dr Smart that about six weeks before the tragedy she had been so ill that she thought she was going to die. The thought then came into her head about what would happen to her boy if she died. He was not strong and could be 'knocked about by the world.' On the morning of the killing something seemed to tell her that she had to do it. The boy had to die before she did. Dr Smart said that he believed all melancholic persons to be suicidal, and many homicidal. He thought that Mrs Cameron, if left to herself, would have committed suicide. She spoke to him as if she had done a good deed in killing her son. When the doctor saw Mrs Cameron, he did not believe she was sane.

Defence counsel Mr Madden pointed out that Louisa Cameron believed she was justified in killing her son. She loved her child, who was simpleminded. She could not bear the thought of herself dying and leaving the poor little fellow to struggle with the world. The jury's verdict was 'guilty but insane'. The judge directed Mrs Cameron to be detained in an asylum for an indefinite period.

Unemployment and the strain on family life

The system of casual employment was not unique to Liverpool, but it did form a very significant part of the labour market in the city. Men would be employed for a half day's work, chosen by foremen either in the morning or in the early afternoon. It was a system that suited employers as it could accommodate the uneven flow of ships and cargoes coming into and going out of the docks; men would be hired only when they were needed. During periods of cyclical economic depression, such as in 1906, many found themselves unable to obtain any work, or only a small amount, insufficient to meet family needs. A couple of cases in this volume note that the accused had suffered periods of unemployment and that this had put a strain on him and his relationships with others.

The sea was another major source of employment in Liverpool, and it is said that most families in the city have members who served on ships as Able Seamen (ABs) or on some of the great liners that regularly sailed the Atlantic.

The nature of both these forms of employment had consequences for wives and families. Wives of the casually employed had to deal with an income that could fluctuate from week to week; wives of seamen had to cope with long periods where they did not see their husbands and lived on part of his wages paid to them by the company he was working for. The pawnbrokers or moneylenders were turned to in order to tide a family over until the next wage packet came in – the wife was expected to cope and manage the family income. A downturn in trade and long-term unemployment combined with poor housing and disease would be enough to drive anybody to drink, despair and ultimately to violence. The strained relationships probably caused by these factors can be seen in several of the cases here.

A Widnes Tragedy

In Edwardian days, before an accused prisoner came to trial at the assizes, the evidence against him was heard and considered by a grand jury, under the supervision of the presiding assize judge. More often than not the grand jury took the advice of the judge when deciding whether or not a defendant should be put on trial. However, on occasions, the grand jury returned a 'true bill' against the prisoner even when the judge believed that the evidence was insufficiently strong to secure a conviction. This happened on 1 March 1908 in the case of John Byrne, who was charged with killing his wife Rose Ann Byrne at Widnes on 3 November 1907. Mr Justice Ridley advised the grand jury to throw out the case. He said to them: 'There is no strong conviction in my mind that guilty can be brought home to the prisoner and if you do not think there is a probability of a conviction it is your duty to throw it out'. However, the grand jury, which consisted of 22 wealthy and influential Liverpool men, with its foreman John Formby of Formby Hall, returned a true bill against John Byrne and the trial was arranged for the Spring Assizes which opened that day.

The trial of 63-year-old John Byrne for murder opened at Liverpool on Friday 6 March 1908 before Mr Justice Ridley and an all-male, twelve-man jury. Byrne was a chemical worker who lived at 18 Brown Street in Moss Bank, near the St Helens canal and the Mersey. When prosecuting counsel the Hon. John Mansfield stood up to address the jury, he admitted that there was not a strong motive for the crime nor evidence of any planning of the murder by Byrne. The case against Byrne, outlined by Mr Mansfield, was circumstantial in nature and there were no eyewitnesses to the killing. The jury was required by Mr Mansfield to try to fit together a series of indirect points of evidence in order to reach a guilty verdict against Byrne.

Although Rose Ann Byrne was addicted to drink, John Byrne had the reputation of being a hard-working man, although on Saturday nights it was no unusual thing for the couple to have a row. On Saturday 2 November 1907, Byrne left his work and went into a pub where he found his wife. They went home together and she had some more beer. They seemed to be on friendly terms, even though they had both drunk quite a lot. They were last seen at about 10.30 that night, when they were on their way home to 18 Brown Street.

No. 16 Brown Street was occupied by the Farrell family. In the small hours of Sunday morning they heard the sounds of quarrelling in the

Byrnes' house. One of them heard a man say: 'You will have to clear out of here and let me rest.' After that was heard a series of banging noises. One of the Farrells described it as the noise of someone going to the back of the house. Others said it sounded like someone running downstairs.

Downstairs, in the kitchen of No. 18, a lodger lay asleep. His name was Thomas Costello and on the Saturday night he was very drunk. Apparently Costello did not know what time he got home that night. At all events, he was awakened in what he called 'the morning side of night' by Byrne coming into the room where he slept and asking for a drink. Costello had some whisky in his pocket and he gave Byrne some. At that time the room was lit up by gas, although Costello could not recollect whether or not the gas was burning when he went to bed.

A few minutes before 6.00 a.m., William Twigg of 22 Brown Street was coming home from work along the street. As he passed the door of No. 18, he came upon Mrs Byrne. She was lying on the pavement with her head towards the kerbstone and her feet pointing towards the wall and window of No. 18, clad only in her chemise. At that time the gaslight was burning in the kitchen and the window of the first floor room above the kitchen was slightly open.

A neighbour called Thomas Wright had passed Byrne's house at about 1.45 a.m. There was no body on the pavement then and no light in the kitchen. After trying in vain to rouse the household at No. 18, Mr Twigg went to get a policeman. Police Constable Hill arrived and examined Mrs Byrne. She was dead, severely wounded over the right temple. Her face was lying in a pool of congealed blood. Efforts were again made to awake the occupants, but without success. PC Hill, with Mr Twigg's help, managed to break down the door.

The lodger Costello lay awake on a sofa. Ann Wright from No. 20 was woken by the knocking and she went upstairs to Byrne's room, crying out: 'John, Rose is dead. She had gone through the window again.' To that, Byrne replied: 'Who put her through?' Mrs Wright said: 'Not me. You if anybody.' Byrne said: 'I am as innocent as a babe unborn. I never missed her out of bed until now.' A few minutes later, Byrne came downstairs and said to PC Hill: 'I wonder where she was. I was downstairs sometime this morning and I had a drink. She was not in bed then. I went back to bed and must have fallen asleep again. I did not waken again until Ann Wright told me about this.' Later in the morning, Byrne said to Mrs Wright:

'Wasn't I asleep when you came up?' Mr Wright replied that 'No, you were as awake as I am'. In his first statement Byrne had said that he missed his wife for the first time when Mrs Wright called to him. To the policeman he said he missed her out of bed when he went downstairs to get a drink. Later on, Byrne made another statement to the police. He said: 'We went home together and I went to bed, and knew nothing more until I was knocked up the following morning about 6 o'clock'. By that time, having an opportunity to consider the matter, Byrne evidently thought it advisable to revert to the statement he originally made to Mrs Wright. Mr Mansfield said to the jury: 'That is a circumstance you will have to consider very seriously because it shows that Byrne had some object in concealing the fact that he had been downstairs during the night.'

Another point was that the house key, which used to be kept by Mrs Byrne, was found lying beside the bed upon which John Byrne had been sleeping. A further incident, to which the jury were asked to give careful attention, was that when Byrne came downstairs after being roused he wore a short-sleeved singlet, and he said to the constable as he came down: 'Where is my shirt?' Hill replied: 'Where did you put your shirt?' To this question, Byrne gave no answer. An hour or so later, Byrne sent a little boy to borrow a shirt from a Mrs McDonald, who lent him one. That was something Byrne had never done before. Subsequently, Byrne's shirt was found lying on an old sofa in the back yard, but there was no evidence to show whether it had been washed or not.

There was a suggestion that Mrs Byrne may have fallen through the front room window onto the pavement. That window was opened at the bottom, but when measurements were taken next day, it was found to be jammed – it could not be opened either way. When measured it was found to be open 13 inches. In front of it, upon a trestle, stood a box. The space between the top of the box and the bottom of the window was only 9 inches. Mrs Byrne was a bulky woman and the depth of her torso as measured by the medical men was 9½ to 10 inches, so it was a physical impossibility for her to have got through a gap of 9 inches. Furthermore, on the box was a cover and a sandbag, both undisturbed. In addition, there was an accumulation of dust which was also undisturbed. She could not have met her death by falling through the window.

The wound on Mrs Byrne's temple was sufficient to have killed her and there was no doubt that it did so, because her skull was fractured. There were other marks of violence on her face and bruises on her arms. The fatal wound might have been inflicted by a heavy blunt instrument and several hammers were found in the home. The doctors agreed that if a fall had caused death, the body would have been found in a different position. They further agreed that all the bruises could not have been caused by a fall. There must have been violence apart from the fatal blow. Several hours elapsed before any search of the house was made, so there would have been ample time to remove any instrument which might have been used.

After the presentation of the case for the prosecution, defence counsel Mr Sandbach submitted that the evidence was insufficient to form any case against Byrne. Questioned by the judge, Mr Mansfield said he could not put the case higher than he had put it in his opening, which was that 'there was no alternative except the hypothesis that the deceased had died at the hands of the prisoner'. The judge said: 'I don't think that will do. You must bring it nearer home.' Mr Mansfield replied: 'The prisoner was in a position in which he could inflict the injury and either carry or follow the woman downstairs. Either would be perfectly consistent with what the people next door heard. The only other hypothesis has been shown to be physically impossible. I cannot, however, carry the case further in the matter of affirmative evidence.'

'I think you ought to bring it much more closely home before you ask for a verdict of murder.'

'If your lordship is of that opinion, I don't think I ought to press the case.'

'I don't know what the jury think', said the judge. 'I think the evidence is not sufficient.'

After a brief consultation, the jury returned a verdict of not guilty and Byrne was discharged.

⁂ 1908 ⁂

Murder at Burscough

On Wednesday 22 July 1908 there opened at St George's Hall the trial of Herbert Gregory Loens, 25, a clerk. He was charged on a coroner's warrant with the wilful murder of Joseph Martland on 11 July at Burscough Bridge. He was also charged with the manslaughter of Martland. To both indictments the accused, a smartly dressed young fellow, pleaded not guilty.

Martland had been a dealer in hay and straw. He was about 50, had retired from business, and was living in a house under a mile from the Royal Hotel, where he received the fatal wound. Loens used to be in the Royal Army Ordnance Corps, stationed at Burscough. He had gone into the Army Reserve in February 1907 and then got work as a ship's clerk, making passages to and from America. While living at Burscough he was accused of fathering a child by a girl who worked in the post office. He did not believe he was the father of the child and his temper was aroused as soon as anyone mentioned the word 'stamps'.

On 11 July 1908, while he was living at Seaforth, Loens decided to have a really good time. It was a Saturday and he went over to Burscough. At 2.00 p.m. he was at the Cambridge Hotel and between that time and 8.30 p.m. he had ample opportunity to take a great deal of drink at the Cambridge and the Royal Hotel. Loens said he heard a man called Woods making some insulting remarks which he thought applied to him. Loens said: 'We had some words, and as a result I went to the back of the house. I pulled a revolver out of my pocket and, swinging it in my hand, said "It's about time some of these insults were stopped. I have had about enough of them". I then put my revolver in my hip pocket and went into the hotel and Woods followed. I said to him: "Would you have a drink with me?" and he had a drink.' Loens explained that the revolver happened to be in his pocket because he had put on his shore suit and had got it as a present from a friend in Montreal. It was given to him because on one occasion he was attacked by footpads, and he therefore kept the weapon in the hip pocket of his shore suit.

Loens went to the Royal Hotel later in the evening. There, among others, was Joseph Martland. He was in the snug and had had a small amount of drink but he was sober. Loens remained standing near the serving bar in the vestibule and while he was drinking there, Martland came out. Giving his version of events, Loens said this:

> I think I was in there about three-quarters of an hour and had four drinks. Shortly after eight o'clock I saw Martland. I was standing by the service window when Martland came out of the little room. I didn't know him or his name. He said, 'Hello, how is stamps getting on?' That expression referred to a girl in the post office who had fathered a child on me. Someone tittered and I lost my temper. Immediately I turned on him and said 'Look here, old cock, I have had just about enough of this, and if it is not stopped I will put three-quarters of an ounce of lead into your head'. While saying this I drew the revolver. I could have fired five chambers into Martland if I had any intention of doing so. Someone sprang on me from behind and pulled my arms down. Then the revolver exploded. I say that the jerking down of my arm was the cause of the revolver exploding. I had no intention whatever of hurting Martland or anyone else. I produced the revolver to frighten him.

Nearby witnesses saw Loens point the weapon at Martland. Martland collapsed and was taken to Dr Gardener's surgery where an operation was performed. He appeared to be progressing comfortably but died on the Sunday afternoon.

Edward Woods of Westhoughton was in the Cambridge Hotel between 5.30 p.m. and 6.30 p.m. He said that Loens came in and accused him of speaking about him. Woods denied it and said he didn't know him. Loens produced a revolver and pointed it at him. In cross-examination, Woods admitted saying 'If the cap fits, wear it'.

John Smith of Burscough was in the Royal Hotel. He saw Loens standing by the bar window at about 8.15 p.m. He was drinking. About 8.30 p.m. Martland came out of the snug. As he passed Loens, Smith heard Loens say something about 'stamps' but did not catch the remark. Loens drew a revolver and threatened, 'I will put three leads in your head'. Loens pointed the gun at Martland's head and Smith seized him. After holding Loens for a few seconds, the gun went off. Martland walked away and Smith followed. Outside the hotel, Martland collapsed. Smith was praised for this conduct by the judge, Mr Justice Bucknill.

John Royle, a saddler from Burscough, said that Martland approached Loens saying 'Hello Stamps'. Loens said: 'Look here, old cock, I won't let you or anyone call me "Stamps", or if you do ...' Here Loens put his hand in his hip pocket and pointed something at Martland, who struck out at Loens. Next, Smith seized hold of Loens. John Lea, a local tradesman, also saw Martland strike out at Loens.

The revolver was of an American make. Two pulls both cocked and then fired the weapon. The judge said that this design was 'to the prisoner's advantage'. Martland made a death bed statement at Dr Gardener's house on the Saturday night in which he said Loens pulled off his coat and hit him. He did not know Loen's name and had never seen him before in his life.

Loens was a native of Gravesend and was educated at the grammar school until he was sixteen. After that, his father took him to live in Belgium. When his father died, Loens carried on his business at Gravesend for a time. He then went to sea as a steward, and then he enlisted in the Army Ordnance Corps. He was transferred to the Army Reserve. According to all reports, Loens had throughout his career borne an excellent character.

In his final remarks for the defence, Mr H. L. Riley said that Loens was not guilty of manslaughter. It was an accident. He said: 'It may be true that the levelling of the revolver was an unlawful act, but to interpret the law on the point, the jury must look both at the words used at the moment and at the whole conduct, of which the levelling of the revolver was a part. I suggest that the levelling was a conditional threat – a demonstration of force of what Loens would do if further insults were levelled at him.' Mr Riley continued: 'It was the well-meant action of Smith which brought about a terrible result. Smith, I contend, acted in unfortunate ignorance of what might happen if he tackled a man with a firearm in his hand.'

Mr Justice Bucknill, summing up, said it was 'altogether a sad case'. He said: 'This young man, who up to this occurrence possessed a high character, has played the fool. Although there clearly was an assault in law, there was a disclaimer of any intention on the part of this prisoner to do harm. It is further suggested that acts on the part of others may have caused the explosion of the revolver. There are some grounds, therefore, which may justify the jury in coming to the conclusion that the prisoner is not guilty of the offence of manslaughter.'

After a brief absence from court, the jury returned a verdict of not guilty of manslaughter. No evidence was presented on the murder charge. Mr Justice Bucknill then delivered a censure against Herbert Loens. He said to him:

> I want to say a word to you, young man. I quite understand the verdict of the jury. I don't want to add to your mental trouble. To the end of your life, I suppose you will never forget this act – how foolish it was, and how wrong it was, to go about this country, where life is not in danger, carrying a loaded revolver in your pocket, and how still more foolish to be in such a hurry to produce it and point it at people – without which this would never had happened. You must remember that in a sense you have to some extent been morally responsible for this poor fellow's death and for the mourning of his widow and children. For the future, make up your mind to walk the country like a man. If people assault you, use your fists, but don't go about with a loaded revolver in your pocket especially when, according to your own statement, you are a man who is prone to be quick-tempered and excitable. Lastly, if it is a fact that on this night you took more drink than was good for you, remember the folly of it. Take what is good for you and no more. Now you can go.

Another Death at Lyons Street, Bootle

On Monday 14 December 1908 at St George's Hall before Mr Justice Channell and a jury, there opened the trial of John Trench, accused of murdering six-year-old Thomas Foy at Bootle some time between 24 and 26 October 1908.

The evidence against Trench was circumstantial, but compelling. It was detailed to the jury by Crown counsel Mr Hogg. Trench's family and Thomas Foy's family all lived in Lyons Street in Bootle. and the boy's body was found at number 71. His father was a coal heaver. On the night of Saturday 24 October, Mr Foy took the boy out to do some shopping. At about 9.40 p.m. the father left him in Derby Road, at the top of Lyons Street. The next that was seen of Tommy was between 10.00 and 10.30 p.m., when he was noticed in

Derby Road, walking along with Trench. They both went into a shop, where Trench bought two meat pies. They then walked off in the direction of Liverpool. That was the last that was seen of the boy alive.

Mr Hogg said that Trench's movements on the Saturday night were of importance. He lived with his parents at 77 Lyons Street. On the afternoon of 24 October, he was with Tommy Foy's elder brother Peter and a man called O'Shaughnessy. They were drinking together. During the evening, Trench, along with Peter Foy and a young man called William Nolan, were drinking in a pub called the Old Toll Bar. All three left the pub between 10.00 and 10.30 p.m. – most likely at 10.15 p.m. The prosecution suggested that Trench went straight away, met the boy, and then went off with him to the shop. The distance from the Old Toll Bar to the shop in Derby Road was about 400 yards. After Trench left them, Peter Foy and Nolan walked about until after 11.00 p.m. They met Mrs Foy, who in the meantime had missed Tommy and told the two men. Foy and Nolan searched the streets but could find no trace of the boy.

They were returning along Lyons Street when something important happened. The houses in Lyons Street were divided into two parts – a cellar part and the upper part, occupied by different tenants and having no access to each other. The upper part of 71 Lyons Street was occupied by a family named McQuirk, while the cellar part had been condemned by the authorities. Its door was locked and the window was boarded up. At about midnight, Peter Foy and Nolan were passing McQuirk's house when they stopped to listen to some singing. Afterwards, their attention was caught by something that was happening in the condemned cellar below. Firstly they heard the sound of someone moaning. Then they heard a sound like snoring, as if someone had got his hand over somebody else's mouth. Nolan kicked the window to try to disturb whoever was in the cellar. There was then the sound of someone scuffling through bricks, which were later found on the cellar floor. The two youths were alarmed by this and went to the back of the house, where there was a passage three feet wide with high walls, giving no access to the houses in Lyons Street. On the entry side the wall was six feet high and on the yard side of 71 Lyons Street the wall was 8 ft 4 in high. Peter Foy had begun to climb the wall of 71, when a bottle was thrown – apparently over the wall of 71 into the entry. It was followed by another mysterious bottle. Both bottles fell into the entry. The youths, feeling they were on a perilous mission, left the entry and returned to Lyons Street. This was about 12.30 a.m. They stood talking for some time and then Trench appeared in the street.

Trench had not been seen since he left the pork shop with Tommy Foy between 10.00 and 10.30 p.m. He was then wearing a dark jacket and blue dungarees. Peter Foy and William Nolan had a few moments conversation with Trench and then they continued their search for the boy along different streets. At 2.30 a.m. they returned to the Foy's house, where Nolan slept on the sofa in the kitchen.

On the Sunday morning, an extraordinary incident occurred. Mr Foy, who had returned home on the Saturday night somewhat the worse for drink, was lying in bed upstairs. At about 8.30 a.m., Trench rushed into the house, ran upstairs, opened the door of Mr Foy's bedroom and cried out: 'Mr Foy, Mr Foy, your little Tommy has been found murdered with his head half off him!' Trench then ran downstairs. As he was going out of the house he met Mrs Foy, to whom he said: 'Good Jesus, Mrs Foy. Is that true that your boy has been found murdered in a cellar, with the head half off him?' Mrs Foy did not attach any importance to what Trench said – although it was strictly true – and she told him to shut up and not to spread such rumours. She added that she was going to the children's shelter and expected to find her boy there. However, she asked Trench who had told him about the cellar. He replied: 'One of the young Monteiths.'

The Monteiths were a family living at 73 Lyons Street. The family consisted of father, mother, and two young girls aged 14 and 9. Both girls denied ever having told Trench about the boy's body being found in the cellar. In fact, they knew nothing about it until long afterwards.

After calling at the Foys' house on the Sunday morning, Trench accosted a barber in Stanley Road and said to him: 'Have you heard the news? A child has been murdered in a cellar in Lyons Street.'

On the Sunday afternoon, Trench was with Peter Foy. In the course of conversation about Tommy's disappearance, Trench said: 'I'll tell you what we'll do. We'll get some candles, start from the top and search all the empty cellars in Lyons Street.' To this, Foy said: 'No, I cannot climb those walls, let alone a boy.' Trench went on to say that he had seen the boy on the previous night with 'two foreigners'. Foy asked: 'Why didn't you chase him home?' Trench then said that he thought he saw the boy 'on a foreigner's knee, taking a penny from him'.

On the Monday, Peter Foy and the other young men started a systematic search of the empty cellars in Lyons Street. They took candles and got over the back wall of No. 71. Access to the cellar was easy, because its back door had been taken away, and in the cellar they found the little boy. He was lying dead, his hands raised as if to guard his head from a blow. His head had been brutally battered. A doctor would say that 'his head half cut off him' accurately described the lad's condition in the eyes of a non-medical man. Dr Stitt, the Bootle police surgeon, was of the opinion that the boy had at first been taken over the back wall. There was some evidence that the boy cried, because a neighbour, whose window almost overlooked the cellar of 71, heard a noise about 11.30 p.m. on Saturday night, as if something had dropped into the yard of 71, followed by a slight scream. It seemed as if the boy had screamed, and the murderer had then hit him on the mouth, knocking him down and causing a slight injury to the boy's head. Then, apparently, the murderer proceeded to batter the boy's face with a scaler's hammer.

The young men took the boy's body to the parents' house. When it was found, the body was clothed, with the exception of the trousers. On the same night, the police arrested Trench at his own house. His brother asked him what the police wanted him for. Trench replied: 'I know. It's Monteith's girl.' In the room was a jacket and a vest. The jacket was the one that Trench had been wearing on the Saturday night. It must have been washed very recently because on that Monday night it was still soaking wet. On the following day, Trench was charged with the murder of the boy. He answered: 'It's not me.'

On 17 November, Mrs Foy and Mrs Monteith visited John Trench and spoke to him at Walton Gaol. Mrs Foy said to Trench: 'Where did you pick up Tommy that Saturday night?' He said, 'At Blackledge's'. She asked: 'Where did you take him to?' Trench replied: 'Over to the pork shop.' In reply to further questions, Trench said he took the boy along Lower Bank View and then let him go home. Mrs Monteith inquired: 'Which of my girls told you the boy was dead?' 'It was either Maggie or Aggie. Anyhow, I saw your big one over at Mrs McGuinness's between 9.30 and 10.00.' It was true that one of the Monteith girls had gone across the road to Mrs McGuinness's to get back a pan her mother had lent. However, Trench had told Mrs Foy the story of the boy lying in the cellar as early as 8.30 a.m. on the Sunday, and the police found a scaler's hammer in the ash pit of the house at which Trench lived.

Concluding his remarks, Crown counsel Mr Hogg told the jury: 'There can be no side door to your verdict. It must be either one of "guilty of wilful murder" or the prisoner's complete acquittal.' After the Crown evidence had been given, the trial adjourned for the day.

The next morning, John Trench went into the witness box to be questioned by defence counsel Mr Griffiths. Trench said that on 24 October, after drinking with Peter Foy, Nolan and others, he went into Derby Road. Just as he was going into the pork shop, he met Tommy Foy. He bought two meat pies. He gave one to the boy and asked him where his brother was. After giving Tommy the pie, he told him to go home. The boy went away and Trench walked home. After a while he went out again for a walk. While out he met Peter Foy and Nolan. Peter asked him for a cigarette and then they all went on to the dock road. There they saw two foreigners who were fighting with a woman about some money. Trench said he then left Nolan and Foy and 'walked about'. Later on, he again met them – in Lyons Street outside the cellar. Nolan said to him: 'Don't make a noise, John. Go and listen, there is someone in there.' Trench said that he suggested that all three of them should go to the back of the house, but Nolan said 'No, it might be our Rose Ann'. Trench said he stayed with them until Nolan went off to Mrs Murphy's house. He then went home.

In evidence, Trench said that next morning, the Sunday, at about 9.30 a.m., he was awakened by somebody in the street shouting out that young Tommy Foy had been found cut up in an empty cellar. He said he looked through the window and saw a girl. He took her to be one of the Monteith girls. He dressed himself and went to the house of the boy's parents. He asked Mr Foy: 'Is that true about your child being found in the cellar cut up?' Mr Foy said: 'No, who told you that?' He answered that he had heard one of the Monteith girls shouting out across the street. As Trench was leaving the house, he met Mrs Foy. He asked her: 'Is it true about your Tommy?' She said: 'What do you mean?' He then told her one of the Monteith girls had shouted it. She replied: 'Someone is trying to have a mark out of you', and she began to laugh.

Trench was then cross-examined by prosecuting counsel Hogg. Mr Hogg asked Trench: 'What did you want to go home for after leaving the Old Toll Bar?'

'Can't I go home when I like?' answered Trench. 'I went home to see how my father and mother were getting on.'

'Why did you ask the boy at the pork shop where his brother was?'

'Because he had been with me all day.'

'That is the only reason?'

'Yes.'

Trench said he was the worse for drink on the Saturday night. He could not suggest any reason why Peter Foy and Nolan should tell lies about him, except it was owing to the fact that they were as drunk as he was on the Saturday night. They had all been drinking together since 3.00 p.m. When he, Foy and Nolan went on to the dock road, after he had been to the pork shop, they saw Tommy Foy sitting on a foreigner's knee. Peter Foy told the boy to go home. Mr Hogg asked: 'I thought you said the foreigners were fighting with a woman about some money?'

'So they were,' replied Trench. 'The little boy was sitting on the step just then.'

The judge asked Trench why the girl's shouting did not cause a commotion in the street, and Trench said he saw no one else in the street. Mr Hogg asked him: 'Why didn't you go out and ask for particulars from the girl?'

'Certainly not,' replied Trench. 'Did you want me to be going after another woman's child?'

The jury were out from 2.00 p.m. until 4.00 p.m., when they returned a verdict of 'not guilty'. Fearing a hostile demonstration against him, Trench's friends hurriedly put him into a taxicab which sped away from St George's Hall.

~ 1909 ~

Oakes Street

Denis Smith, a 52-year-old Auctioneer's porter, lived with his wife Sarah Ann Smith at their home at 9 in No. 2 Court, Oakes Street, off London Road. Also living at the house was their son Joseph (12) and their nephew Owen (8).

On 9 February 1909, Smith, who had consumed a good deal of drink during the day, reached his home about 3.30 p.m. There he continued drinking with his wife and a neighbour. He sent his wife out two or three times for more beer. Later, he sent her to buy food for his tea. When Sarah Ann returned with some fish, Smith upbraided her for being away so long, whereupon Mrs Smith refused to cook the meal. A quarrel erupted.

Their quarrel ended with the woman running out of the house screaming 'Murder!' and Smith chasing her in his stockinged feet. He then lay down on his bed and slept for a while. Mrs Smith cooked the fish while he slept. When she woke him for the meal he refused it. He said it was hardly cooked, the quarrel was resumed and abusive names were exchanged. Finally, Smith, jumping up from the bed, picked up a dinner knife from the table. Shouting 'I will fix you!' he struck his wife under the left ear. She bled profusely. Smith tried to staunch the bleeding with a towel, and carried her onto a sofa. 'I didn't mean to do it', he cried. His wife replied: 'It is what you have always been threatening.' Smith and his son took Mrs Smith across Pembroke Place to the Royal Infirmary. She died there after a few minutes.

Because his shirt was saturated in blood, Smith was allowed to go home to change his clothes. He did not go back to the infirmary. Instead, later in the night, he was seen walking down Islington, wringing blood from a cloth – presumably the shirt he wore at the time of the attack. When he was arrested at his sister's house he was wearing a fresh shirt. While at the infirmary, Smith's son said: 'She did it herself.'

Oakes Street.
Liverpool Record Office, Liverpool Libraries and Information Services

Denis Smith's trial for murder was held at Liverpool Assizes on Thursday 11 March 1909. The judge was the Lord Chief Justice, Lord Alverstone. The main witness against Smith was his son Joseph, and the boy broke down repeatedly while giving his evidence. Resting his head on his arms on the ledge of the box, he cried bitterly. Smith too was deeply moved. In cross examination, Mr Riley the defence counsel, suggested that the woman's injury had been inflicted accidentally by Smith trying to pull her to the table while he was holding the knife in his hand. The boy's testimony, however, did not bear this out.

During his summing up Lord Alverstone told the jury it would be unsafe to find Smith guilty of murder, 'having regard to the absence of motive and the obvious remorse which Smith exhibited after the occurrence'.

Mr Riley then changed Smith's plea to 'guilty of manslaughter' – which, on the direction of the judge, the jury so found. Mr Riley then called evidence of Smith's good character. It was said that Smith's home was 'wretchedly kept, only one room out of four being furnished'. During the last eighteen months, the wife had been drunk 'three or four times a week'. The judge said he recognised that Smith's act was 'unpremeditated and the result of sudden irritation'. He sentenced Smith to seven years penal servitude.

Burlington Street Child Murder

On 26 January 1909, fireman William McCormick came home to his house in Burlington Street, off Vauxhall Road. It was about 5.30 p.m. His elder child, a boy of five years, was leaving the house to play in the street. McCormick recalled the boy and sent him up to bed. Standing in the doorway of the house was his younger son John Patrick, aged 19 months. McCormick picked him up and carried him upstairs in his arms.

A few minutes later, the elder child came running down the stairs, bleeding from the neck. His grandmother carried him out into the street and began to scream out: 'Murder!' A neighbour and a police officer arrived on the scene. She told them what had happened and they went into the house, where they found McCormick sitting at a table with a razor in his hand. The baby lay dead on the floor, with its throat cut. When the policeman spoke to McCormick he replied: 'I have killed two of them. I meant to do it.'

When he reached the bridewell, McCormick asked the police officer to take down a statement. It read: 'The blood of my own kids is on my hands. I could not keep or rear them. I intended to commit murder. I am not insane or mad.'

McCormick came to trial at the Liverpool Spring Assizes on 11 March 1909. Opening the case for the prosecution, Mr Hogg said that the jury would have to consider McCormick's mental condition at the time he committed the fatal act. Both he and his wife were of steady habits, said Mr Hogg. Mrs McCormick's mother was living with them. The household had been a happy one. McCormick had been a marine fireman. Eighteen months earlier he met with an accident to his leg. Since then he had experienced difficulty in passing the doctor for a sea-going job. Since the accident he had been on three voyages only.

Burlington Street.
Liverpool Record Office, Liverpool Libraries and Information Services

According to the police, immediately after the murder McCormick seemed rational. On the instructions of the Director of Public Prosecutions he had been kept under observation at the gaol. At the trial, both his wife and his mother-in-law testified to his depression after his accident.

Evidence came from Dr A. E. Davis, who saw McCormick at Walton Gaol. McCormick had told the doctor something of his history. Four years ago, McCormick jumped overboard from a steamer in Lyttleton Harbour, New Zealand, and was kept for some time in the hospital there. He could give no reason for doing that. On another occasion, said McCormick, he jumped into a Liverpool dock and was nearly drowned. Again he could offer no explanation for his conduct. When McCormick was young, he and his brothers had to live in the best way they could. Sometimes they had to steal. The accident eighteen months before, and the difficulties in which it placed him, had preyed very much on McCormick's mind. He was upset by the idea that his children might have to go through the same terrible experience as he and his brothers had undergone. He began to wonder whether it might not be better for them if they were dead. In Dr Davis's opinion, McCormick was the victim of a sort of 'explosive insanity' or of 'impulsive insanity' brought about by melancholia. At intervals, he was perfectly sane.

Dr Price, Chief Medical Officer at Walton, said that in his opinion

McCormick was mentally sound. He said that if what Dr Davis had related of McCormick's story were true, he agreed that there was 'a tendency to impulsive action or action without thought'. Dr Price said he had considered witnesses' statements and it did not appear to him that McCormick had acted on a sudden impulse.

The jury returned a verdict of 'guilty but insane' and McCormick was detained as a criminal lunatic.

Dickenson Street

Another case tried at the 1909 Liverpool Spring Assizes before Lord Chief Justice Alverstone involved two Chinese sailors. A man called See Lee was accused of shooting to death another Chinaman called Yang Yap in a house in Dickenson Street on 4 December 1908.

See Lee and Yang Yap had known each other for about a year. They were both friendly with a woman called Amy Yap Sing, the English wife of a Chinaman who had returned to China. The woman had been laid up in bed with peritonitis and both See Lee and Yang Yap used to visit her in her bedroom. The two men often met on these visits and they were on friendly terms with each other.

On 4 December Yang Yap called to see Mrs Sing at about 9.00 p.m. After he had been there for a little while, somebody was heard coming upstairs. At the woman's request Yang Yap went to the top of the stairs to see who it was. He called out 'It is See Lee', and returned to the bedroom. A moment later, See Lee entered and, without uttering a word, fired a revolver at Yang, who fell across the bed. 'What have you done to poor old Sukie?' cried the woman. See Lee did not answer. He walked out of the room. As he was leaving the house, he met a woman called Mrs Harris. He smiled at her as he passed, but said nothing.

While a search was being made for a policeman, Yang crawled downstairs from the bedroom to the kitchen. The revolver used was never found but Yang, who was shot in the left side, died three days later from septic poisoning of his wound.

See Lee was arrested at Lime Street station and he said he had intended

The corner of Dickenson Street and Pitt Street.
Liverpool Record Office, Liverpool Libraries and Information Services

going to Glasgow and then to Cardiff. At the police station he volunteered this statement: 'Yang Yap was jealous of me and Mrs Yap Sing. When I went upstairs he was sitting on the chair. He took the revolver out of his hip pocket and pointed it at me. I took it from him and shot him, or he would have shot me.'

Later on, See Lee changed his story to the effect that he had tried to take the pistol from Yang but had failed. In the struggle, the pistol went off and Yang shot himself.

A statement was also taken from Yang Yap in his hospital bed. When he heard See Lee's version of events, he called him a liar. Yang said: 'See Lee didn't speak, but simply shot me with a revolver. I had no revolver. I don't know why he shot me. I have never had a quarrel with him.'

Mrs Yap Sing said she did not see the revolver, but when it was fired Yang Yap reeled and fell across the bed. She had never seen either of the men with a revolver. Two Chinese witnesses, one of whom took the oath by breaking a saucer in the Chinese fashion, testified that Yang Yap was a quiet steady man who did not carry a gun.

Dr Simpson of the Royal Southern Hospital said it was impossible for Yang to have shot himself with his right hand. It would have been extremely awkward to have done so with his left hand. The gun must have been pointed directly at Yang's side.

See Lee himself gave evidence in his own defence. He said he was a Christian and a member of the Church of England. He maintained that Yang Yap produced a revolver from his hip pocket when See Lee entered the room. 'I held his hand and turned it round. I said "Let go! Let go!" and he would not, and he shot himself. I was frightened and I ran away. I had not revolver with me. We were good friends, but I think he was jealous of me.'

After ten minutes' deliberation, the jury found See Lee guilty of wilful murder. He was automatically sentenced to death by Lord Alverstone.

At first, See Lee's solicitor, Mr T. B. Eastley of 37A Manchester Street, said the idea of getting up a petition for the condemned man's reprieve had to all intents and purposes been abandoned. This was announced on Wednesday 17 March. One reason was that the local Chinese community was not unanimous in the matter. If one party got up a petition, there would be a counter-petition to the Home Secretary in favour of hanging. There would be no appeal to the Court of Criminal Appeal.

However, on Thursday 25 March it was reported that a petition for a reprieve had been sent to London from Mr Eastley's office. It was contended that there was no evidence of premeditation of the killing. The execution was fixed for 30 March and on the 27th, Eastley received a letter from the Home Office saying there would be no reprieve.

At 9.00 a.m. on 30 March 1909 See Lee, Chinese sailor and cook, was executed at Walton. The executioner was Harry Albert Pierrepoint, assisted by his brother Thomas William Pierrepoint.

The timespan between sentence and execution on average had been a fortnight. From the late nineteenth century onwards this time was lengthened, and by the turn of the century there was a generally accepted timespan of three clear Sundays. This allowed enough time for any new evidence to come to light which might reverse or commute a sentence. It also made the painful wait for execution no longer than was absolutely necessary.

A Toxteth Servant

Before the crime of infanticide was incorporated into English Law, a woman who disposed of her new-born baby was charged with murder. Such a woman was 30-year-old Alice Amelia Spelman. She came before Mr Justice Walton on Wednesday 28 April 1909, accused of the murder of her infant child on 6 March at a house in Mill Street, Toxteth.

Alice Spelman was single and was a native of Derby. In the summer of 1908 she was in service at a hotel in Llandudno and she came to Liverpool in the October of that year. In December, Alice called at the Samaritan Hospital and told the matron that she was expecting a child, claiming that she was a married woman with three children. Alice called again at the hospital in February. She wanted to know if the matron could help her in any way at the approaching birth. The matron advised her that the best course was to go into the workhouse. Alice was then living in Vine Street.

On 23 February 1909, Alice Spelman was taken on as a general servant in Mill Street. Her mistress suspected she was pregnant but Alice denied it. On the morning of 6 March Alice was taken ill. Her mistress sent for a cab and she was driven away to the Toxteth Workhouse in Smithdown Road. She had with her a basket. When the basket was searched, it was found to contain the dead body of a newly born child. A silk handkerchief was tied around the child's neck and the ends were stuffed into the mouth.

A post mortem showed that the baby had lived, and that it had died by strangulation.

Alice told the police that this was her third child. She was arrested by Detective Sergeant Ford on 25 March and charged with murder. When charged, Alice said, 'I have nothing to say, only that I remember the child being born. That day is blank to me.'

At the trial, after the prosecution case had been presented by Mr Herbert Rathbone, defence counsel Mr Madden told the court that Alice Spelman was left an orphan at the age of five. He urged to the jury that even at the worst, she was guilty only of concealment of birth. He said that the evidence of strangulation was 'inconclusive'. 'A poor friendless woman like the prisoner is entitled to benefit of the doubt', said Mr Madden.

The jury found Alice Spelman guilty of concealing the birth of the child. Mr Justice Walton sentenced her to twelve months imprisonment.

⋆⋙☙⋘⋆

Chesterton Street, Garston

Before Lord Justice Coleridge on 20 July 1909, 24-year-old William Haughton was indicted with the wilful murder of his father William, 57, on Whit Monday, 31 May 1909, at the family home in Chesterton Street, Garston. He was represented in court by Mr Riley. Leading counsel for the Crown was Mr Spencer Hogg.

Outlining his case against Haughton, Mr Hogg said the family consisted of Mr and Mrs Haughton, the accused, who was the eldest of three sons, together with two daughters – Emily (16) and May (14). Mrs Haughton had for a long time been crippled by severe rheumatism. The dead man had been addicted to drink. When in a drunken condition he was often guilty of acts of violence towards his wife and his daughter.

It was usual for Mrs Haughton to sleep in the parlour with the two girls. The father slept in the kitchen, while the three brothers slept upstairs. On Whit Monday, Mr Haughton Senior was the worse for drink. At teatime he was dissatisfied with some cold meat that was given to him so he threw it through the window. Next he picked up a basin, filled it with water, and repeatedly threw the water over his wife while she sat helpless in a chair. He then left the house.

At about 9.00 p.m. that day, the mother and the two girls went to bed. Mr Haughton returned at about 10.00 p.m. and after playing a few tunes on the piano, he too went upstairs to bed. However, at about 11.30 p.m., Mrs Haughton and her two daughters were rudely awakened by Mr Haughton coming into their room and noisily demanding a pair of working trousers. He was drunk and he was shouting all over the house. William came downstairs and told him to be quiet, adding that it was bedtime. The father replied, 'What's that got to do with you?' and struck his son in the face. William retaliated by punching his father twice in the face.

There were two separate versions of what happened next. One version was that after William struck his father, Mr Haughton fell down on the floor and the son reached over him, picked up a poker and hit him four or five times across the head. The second version of events was that after the father was hit by William, he caught hold of him. There was a struggle and both fell. Mr Haughton had his hand on his son's shirt and his knee on his chest. William, who lay on his back, afraid for his life, picked up the poker and hit his father in self-defence.

Mr Hogg said that if the second version was true, the only force exerted by William was from his elbow downwards. He said that there could be no doubt, however, that blows were struck with considerable violence. The father was rendered unconscious and William, who appeared very sorry for what he had done, told his younger brother to go for the police. 'I did it to defend myself', said William to a police officer. 'I am sorry for what I have done. I hit him over the head with the poker five times to prevent him ill-using my mother, who is an invalid. I was upstairs and heard him beating my mother. I at once rushed downstairs and done my best to stop him. He came for me in the kitchen, and to defend myself I did him with the poker over the head.'

Mr Haughton died within a few hours of being admitted to hospital. At the coroner's inquest, William made a statement in which he said he was a total abstainer from alcohol. While admitting to having struck his father, he said he had no intention to kill him or to do him any bodily harm. The post mortem examination showed a skull fracture in two places. The temple bone had been completely shattered.

Young Emily Haughton testified that her father had a violent temper and was addicted to drink. He had often assaulted her mother as well as herself and her sister. Her brother William spent far more money on the house than her father did. Emily said that her father threw William down and put his knee on his stomach. William then picked up the poker and hit his father with it. At the end of Emily's evidence, the judge said it was a question of manslaughter or nothing. Mr Hogg agreed with the judge's ruling. Mary Haughton then corroborated her sister's evidence.

Mr Riley's defence case began with evidence from young William Haughton himself. He said that when he heard his mother screaming, he went down to her room. He saw what his father was doing to her; he was a coward. The father hit William and William hit him back. They closed together and fell down near the fireplace fender, the father uppermost. He pressed his knee into William's chest. William struck his father several times with the poker but he said he was so frightened that he was not now able to remember how many times he struck. He said he had no intention of killing his father or of doing any more than to defend himself. He said also that for some time he had practically kept the household.

Evidence about young William Haughton's character was given by the incumbent Vicar of Garston, the Rev. T. P. Rowe. He gave William an excellent character reference. During the last three years he had been confirmed and had attended church as a communicant. William had been in church both in the morning and in the evening. Mr Rowe said he looked upon him as a very quiet, inoffensive and respectable member of the community.

In his final address, Mr Riley said he believed that the defendant's intervention was not only justified, it was meritorious. 'If the prisoner had not interfered there still might have been an assize trial, but it would not have been this William Haughton who would have figured in the dock.'

Without leaving the court, the jury gave a 'not guilty' verdict. It was greeted by loud applause from the public seats. The judge rebuked the demonstration of delight. He said, 'Simple justice has been done. There is no occasion for applause.' William Haughton was released.

A West Derby Murder

Mr Justice Ridley was the Liverpool Assize judge in November 1909. On the 22nd of that month was heard the trial of Benjamin Scholey, a groom. He was accused of killing a young married woman called Minnie Gascoigne. Leading counsel for the Crown was Mr A. Spencer Hogg. The defence was handled by Mr E. Wooll.

Scholey lived with his mother in Liverpool until he was 17, when he enlisted in the Army Service Corps. Before that time, Mrs Gascoigne, who was then known as Minnie Heard, had been friendly with Scholey. While he was away, however, she married a man called Gascoigne. In September 1909 Scholey got his discharge from the Army and renewed his acquaintance with Minnie. The Crown alleged that Scholey could not persuade Minnie to leave her husband and so he killed her.

In April, Minnie was living with her husband and her two children at 76 Hughes Street in the Liverpool 6 postal district. Up to that time she was a sober industrious woman, fond of her husband and children. One day in June 1909 she brought Ben Scholey to her home and introduced him to her husband as 'an old school chum'. From then on the woman's habits began to change. She took to drink and stayed out late at night.

On 13 July she left home and, until the end of September, Mr Gascoigne could not find her. However, they eventually did live together again at 40 Exley Street. On 1 October, Minnie met Scholey in the morning and stayed out all day. She came home drunk. On the following day, Scholey wanted her to go to Ireland with him, but Minnie said she could not leave her children. On 3 October, she left the house in Exley Street and never returned to it. During that day, Scholey went to a pub where he and Mrs Gascoigne were well known. He was alleged to have said to Mr Boyd, the landlord: 'I am going to do for her. I am going to have her life.' Scholey was drinking heavily. Later on that same day, he was again in the pub. He took from his pocket a case, from which he drew a razor, saying 'I'll kill her when I get hold of her'.

On the morning of Monday 4 October, in a house in Rockwood Street, Scholey said to Mrs Gascoigne: 'Minnie, I love you. It is now coming to a pass. I will kill you.' Shortly afterwards he said to a woman friend of Minnie's: 'She has fooled me for nine years. If she does not come away with me tonight she will not do it any more.'

At 4.30 p.m. on 4 October the couple were seen in West Derby. A labourer called Bill Sumner, who worked on a farm in Norris Green, saw the couple pass along Oak Lane and down Croxteth Hall Lane. From the way Scholey walked, he judged that he was drunk. While in Croxteth Hall Lane, Sumner saw the man and woman struggling, about a hundred yards from a brook which ran under the roadway. He saw Scholey go through a gap in the hedge at one side of the bridge and pull the woman, who was resisting, after him, into a field. This was the last time Sumner saw them. Mr Hogg told the jury: 'There can be no doubt whatever that about that time and at that place, the prisoner took the life of this woman by strangling her with a belt he was wearing.'

Scholey got back to his mother's at about 7.00 p.m. Concerning Minnie Gascoigne, Scholey told his mother that he had 'done for her'. He said he had done it with his belt, showing at the same time that he was not wearing it. Scholey took out some of Minnie's letters and burned them. He said he was quite sure she would never deceive another man. Later that evening, Scholey went to Boyd's pub and said to a coachmen there: 'I have killed Minnie. I strangled her with my belt and left her in a brook in West Derby.'

Shortly afterwards, Scholey was arrested for being drunk and disorderly. As he was being taken to the bridewell he was alleged to have said: 'Don't lock me up for being drunk and disorderly but for murder.' At the police station, Scholey made a statement about Mrs Gascoigne. He said he met her that day at the corner of Butler Street and West Derby Road. They went to Croxteth Hall Lane where, between 4.00 p.m. and 5.00 p.m., he strangled her with a belt. He added: 'She made me do it. She is lying in the brook on the Earl of Sefton's estate. She drove me mad. I know the spot; I can take you to it.'

Detectives hired a cab and drove with Scholey to West Derby. On the way, Scholey said: 'I loved Minnie since I was a little boy. For nine years she drove me mad. From Thursday up till now I have been drinking nothing but whisky.' The police discovered the body after about an hour's search. It lay in the brook under the bridge with Scholey's belt alongside.

Giving evidence in his own defence, questioned by Mr Wooll, Scholey said he had known Minnie Gascoigne for eight years. They had arranged to get married but she married Gascoigne instead. He meant to have nothing more to do with her but she sent him letters. After leaving the Army, he came to Liverpool and they found they were still fond of each other.

Scholey said that on the morning of 4 October he drank between ten and twelve whiskies. From that time his mind was a blank. He did not know what he was doing or saying until he found himself under arrest. He did not remember seeing Mrs Gascoigne that day, nor did he remember going to West Derby. He could not remember speaking to his mother that night either. Mr Wooll asked Scholey: 'Did you want to kill this woman?'

'Certainly not,' replied Scholey.

Dr Price of Walton Gaol said he saw Scholey on 12 October and found him perfectly sane. The doctor did not believe he had been unconscious from whisky on 4 October. In conclusion, Mr Wooll asked the jury for a verdict of temporary insanity. He said: 'The prisoner's insanity was due to excessive alcoholism and the pent-up passion of three years. The Crown are asking the jury to send to the gallows a man whom their own witnesses said could not tell right from wrong.' When Wooll referred to the fascination that Mrs Gascoigne exerted on Scholey, the latter burst into tears.

Summing up, Mr Justice Ridley said that drunkenness was no defence. 'Only an attack of delirium tremens would be a sufficient reply to a charge of murder. That is not borne out in this case', said the judge.

At 6.00 p.m. the jury went out to consider their verdict. They returned to court at 6.40 p.m. The verdict was 'Guilty, with a strong recommendation to mercy on the grounds of Scholey's youth and previous good character'. The judge said: 'The recommendation will be passed to the proper quarter', and then pronounced the death sentence. Scholey walked calmly and firmly out of the dock and stepped down to the cells. His death sentence was later commuted to life imprisonment.

1910

King Edward VII died at 11.45 p.m. on 6 May 1910,
so ending the Edwardian era. However, that period of
England's history is often extended to cover the years
up to the outbreak of the First World War in 1914.

Suggested Further Reading

Aughton, Peter, *Liverpool: A People's History* (Carnegie, 2003)

Brabin, Angela, *The Black Widows of Liverpool: A chilling account of cold-blooded murder in Victorian Liverpool* (Palatine Books, 2003)

Caradog-Jones, *A Social Survey of Merseyside* (3 vols) (Liverpool University Press, 1934)

Fielding, Steve, *The Hangman's Record, Vol. I, 1868–1899* (Chancery House Press, 1994)

Gatrell, V. A. C., *The Hanging Tree: Execution and the English People 1770–1868* (Oxford University Press, 1994)

Hayhurst, Alan, *Lancashire Murders* (Sutton Publishing, 2004)

Jones, Steve, *Lancashire Lasses, their lives and crimes* (Wicked Publications, 2001)

Lane, Tony, *Liverpool Gateway to Empire* (London, 1987)

Lawton, R. and Cunningham, C. M. (eds), *Merseyside Social and Economic Studies* (Longman, 1970)

O'Connor, Freddy, *Liverpool: Our City, Our Heritage* (O'Connor, F., 1990)

O'Mara, Pat, *The Autobiography of a Liverpool Slummy* (The Bluecoat Press, 1994)

Phillips, G. and Whiteside, N., *Casual Labour: The Unemployment question in the Port Transport Industry 1880–1970* (Clarendon Press, 1985)

Sewart, Alan, *Murder in Lancashire: A New Look at Notorious Cases* (Robert Hale, 1988)

Sloan, Tod, *The Treadmill and the Rope: The History of a Liverpool Prison* (Gallery Press, 1988)

Wong, M. L., *Chinese Liverpudlians: A History of the Chinese Community in Liverpool* (Liver Press, 1989)

Woods, J., *Growin' Up: One Scouser's Social History, 1925–1942* (Palatine Books, 2004)